This edition published by:-
Oriental Publications
16 Market Street
Adelaide 5000
South Australia

National Library of Australia Cataloguing-in Publication:-
Bibliography.

ISBN 0 95871132 1

1. Feng Shui. 1. Title.

NORTH AMERICAN EDITION
Published by Oriental Publications
(Under License from Konsep Lagenda Sdn Bhd)
Illustrations and Cover Design by Lillian Too
Copyright: © *1993 Lillian Too*
Printed by Ritz Print Sdn Bhd

First published January 1993
Eight reprints through 1993, 1994 and 1995
This revised new edition January 1996
First reprint of new edition March 1996
Second reprint of new edition September 1997

FENG SHUI

by
Lillian Too

ORIENTAL
PUBLICATIONS

This book is dedicated to my family . . .
To my daughter Jennifer,
To my husband Wan Jin,
To my late father, Lim Bor Yee,
To my mother, Nancy,
To my brothers Phillip & Alex,
To my niece Honey, and my nephew Han Jin

OTHER BOOKS BY THE AUTHOR

FENG SHUI: THE CHINESE DRAGON
APPLIED PA-KUA and LO SHU FENG SHUI
PRACTICAL APPLICATIONS OF FENG SHUI
CHINESE NUMEROLOGY IN FENG SHUI
WATER FENG SHUI FOR WEALTH
EXPLORE THE FRONTIERS OF YOUR MIND
TAP THE POWER INSIDE YOU
CHINESE ASTROLOGY FOR ROMANCE & RELATIONSHIPS

WHY FENG SHUI

Why do some families prosper more than others,
Why does one restaurant flourish,
And another does not...
Why do some companies enjoy robust growth,
While others diminish and weaken...
Why does affluence occur easily for some people,
While ruin and bankruptcy befall others...

The Chinese believe *Feng Shui* offer potent explanations; They believe that positive and negative fortunes arise from auspicious or inauspicious *Feng Shui.*
Today curiosity and interest in this centuries old Chinese wisdom & practice is going through a spectacular revival.

In Hong Kong, Singapore and Taipeh, three of the world's most commercially successful cities, *Feng Shui* is a principal consideration when businessmen build their homes or construct their offices. They believe that getting their *Feng Shui* right will create abundance and prosperity for themselves and their descendants...

With such promise can anyone afford not to know about *Feng Shui* ?

MAN AND HIS ENVIRONMENT
MUST HARMONISE

This is an age old wisdom that advocates equilibrium
and symmetry with the world's landscapes,
its mountains and rivers, its winds and its waters.

The Chinese practice of FENG SHUI encapsulates this in a
broadbased body of principles that promise prosperity and abundance,
peace and serenity, health and longevity to those who live
according to its guidelines of harmony & balance.
It is a beneficial component of Chinese culture.

FENG SHUI is the Chinese Science of Geomancy, and Lillian Too's
books on this centuries old practice is timely and topical.
Certainly the Chinese throughout South East Asia,
Hong Kong & Taiwan are fervent practitioners of FENG SHUI,
especially those in business who want an extra edge in
the form of Feng Shui *luck* .... Like many of my fellow
Malaysians of Chinese origin, I am only too familiar
with the importance of orienting one's home
according to good Feng Shui precepts.

Lillian's books are convincing, thoroughly researched
and extremely comprehensive. Classical explanations
extracted from ancient manuals, are freely interspersed
with hundreds of useful tips and plenty of business
picked up from her many years of business experience.

I am very pleased to recommend "FENG SHUI"
and "APPLIED FENG SHUI" to Malaysians and visitors alike;
for those who want an introduction to the subject, and
for those who want authentic and comprehensive
reference books on the subject.

YB. Datuk Seri Dr. Ling Liong Sik,
President, Malaysian Chinese Association
Minister of Transport,
Government of Malaysia.

WHAT OTHERS SAY ...

*"Lillian Too a corporate high flyer until she called it quits five years ago, has found a fulfilling career in writing. The author of eight best sellers talks about her passion for the ancient Chinese belief of **feng shui** ...... "*
The SUN megazine 25 Nov 1994

*"Too, an ardent believer in **feng shui** lists three types of luck - heaven luck (what God gives you); earth luck (feng shui) and luck which man himself has the power to create .... there was no doubt her audience that day was not only captivated by Too's fluency, wit and humour, but also by her candour and down to earth attitude ..."*
New Straits Times 6 April 1995

*"Lillian Too might be better known to some as the first woman in Asia to head a bank, ... she attributes much of her success to the "science" of **feng shui**. Fully illustrated, her feng shui books plot the development of this ancient practice and offer concise explanations, hints and suggestions for readers to look at their own living and work space. The author's ... clearly written and fascinating books ... are sure to make all who read them look at feng shui with more seriousness and respect"*
Karen Smith in B International, Hong Kong. Sept. 1993

*Highly readable and well illustrated, this book (Applied Pa Kua Lo Shu Feng Shui) will delight you, whether you are a believer or a non believer of **feng shui**"*
Her World August 1993

*Lillian Too's practical, handbook style introduction to **feng shui** gives a simple yet comprehensive overview ... the book is at its best describing diagnosis of problems and offering remedies to improve the feng shui of affected dwellings."*
The Star newspaper 17 Feb. 1993

"Lillian Too believes in the balance and harmony of feng shui ... which she says has been good for her and her family. The lady is something of a legend in Malaysian corporate circles ... and very motivated in her writing ..."
Malaysian Business Nov. 16 1993

*" Having gained esteem and experience in the corporate world quite inaccessible to the ordinary person, she has now turned her hand to writing, and the art of **feng shui** is right up her street...."*
Corporate World Nov. 1993

FENG SHUI

THE DEFINITIVE INTRODUCTORY MANUAL

CONTENTS

FENG SHUI

THE DEFINITIVE INTRODUCTORY MANUAL

CONTENTS

FENG SHUI

THE DEFINITIVE INTRODUCTORY MANUAL

CONTENTS

The Green Dragon is happy, he flies in the clouds,
Good fortune comes continiously. Everything is smooth.

PART ONE

❒ UNDERSTANDING FENG SHUI

From the Chinese Earth, there arise a thousand rich aromas, the most fascinating of which are its divinitive and metaphysical sciences. Feng Shui is probably one metaphysical science which holds out the most extraordinary and exciting promise for Man to consciously rearrange his living space in order to attract all the good fortune that the living Earth offers !

An aura of mysticism surrounds the practice of Feng Shui. Here, we commence penetration of the obscure domains of Chinese symbolism, divination and astrology, covering the whole spectrum of the Chinese preoccupation with Man's relationship with the Universe; a practice which stresses a critical need for balance and harmony.

Feng Shui is the science of living in harmony with the land, such that one derives the greatest benefits, peace and prosperity from being in perfect equilibrium with Nature. Feng Shui holds out the promise of a life of meaningful abundance to those who follow its principles and precepts when building their homes & work places.

Literally, Feng Shui means wind and water.

Many have told me, "Feng Shui is the *wind, which you cannot comprehend, and it is the water which you cannot grasp"*

Wind and water together express the power of Nature's flowing elements, and its effects on surface landscapes. Feng Shui recognises that the Earth's surface is sculpted by wind and water. Feng Shui insists that one needs to live in harmony with the winds the waters of the Earth, if we want these elements to create positive Energy flows that work in our favour. To succeed in doing this we need to place our homes and our working places in locations which are favourable from a Feng Shui perspective. If we succeed, the environment then delivers good fortune, peace, prosperity and abundant good luck into our lives.

Feng Shui cannot be viewed narrowly, either as only a science, with *magical* formulae, nor just as an art based completely on instincts. Feng Shui is a flexible mixture of both. To practice Feng Shui successfully conceptual principles extracted from ancient classical Manuals must be applied in consonance with the thinking Man's common sense and rational judgement.

1

To complicate the practice further, there are also elements of superstitious beliefs that are superimposed on the whole body of principles. These cannot be ignored or forgotten. Indeed symbolism and village type superstition is often employed by today's veterans in their Feng Shui diagnosis, mainly because these so called superstitions represent, in essence, the *word of mouth* journey which feng shui took to travel through the centuries from its origins in ancient times ! Much of the more simple aspects of the practice have been passed down from father to son, and over time these practices have taken on cultural and superstitious overtones.

Understanding Feng Shui in depth however, requires comprehensive knowledge of the philosophical principles that make up the mainstay of Chinese beliefs and Chinese culture, i.e. concepts of harmony and balance, Yin and Yang, the I Ching and the Pa Kua; the five elements, and most important of all, understanding the concept of *CHI*, the vital cosmic breath of the Dragon.

2. HISTORY AND BACKGROUND

Feng Shui has been practised in China at least since the Tang Dynasty. The most ancient master in this art, **Yang Yun Sang**, is universally acknowledged as the Founder of Feng Shui. Master Yang left a legacy of classics that have been preserved and continuously studied to this day. He was the principal advisor at the Court of the Emperor Hi Tsang (AD888), and his books on Feng Shui made up the major texts on which succeeding generations of practitioners based their knowledge. Master Yang's emphasis was on the shape of the mountains, the direction of water courses, and above all, on locating and understanding the influence of the Dragon, China's most revered celestial creature.

Master Yang's theories were detailed in three famous classic works, all of which describe Feng Shui practice in terms of colourful Dragon metaphors. The first of these, "Han Lung Ching" contains the *"Art of Rousing the Dragon"*. The second, "Ching Nang Ao Chih" contains methods of determining the location of the Dragon's lair, while the third book is "I Lung Ching" translated under the title *"Canons approximating Dragons"*.

This tells us how to find the Dragon in areas where they do not prominently stand forth.

Many modern extracts and explanations of the old texts on feng shui can be found in Taiwan where the practice of feng shui is most widespread, and also in Hong Kong. These two countries practice different variations of feng shui, and base their methods on different Schools of thought.

It should not be surprising that there should indeed have evolved several variations and different Schools of thought on a practice that has its origins over three thousand years ago ! Notwithstanding this however it is useful to view Feng Shui as falling under two major Schools of thought, the *Form School* and the *Compass School.*

THE FORM SCHOOL and COMPASS SCHOOL

Master Yang's principles came to be regarded as the *Form School* of Feng Shui, which explains good or bad sites in terms of Dragon symbolism. According to this School, Good Feng Shui locations require the presence of the <u>Dragon</u>, and where there is the true Dragon, there also will be found the <u>White Tiger</u>. Feng Shui Masters of the Form School thus begin their search for good locations by first searching for the Dragon. Emphasis was thus put on landforms, shapes of hills and mountains, waterways, their orientations and directions.

While Dragon symbolism was the principle mainstay of the Form School there eventually emerged a second major system, collectively referred to as the *Compass School.* This second system laid stress on metaphysical speculations and used the *Eight Trigrams* of the I Ching, the eight sided *Pak Kua* symbol, the nine grid *Lo Shu* magic square, the Ghanzhi system of the Chinese calendar which involved understanding of *Heavenly Stems*, and *Earthly Branches* as well as the imaginary constellation of stars that feature strongly in related divinitive sciences.

Compass School Feng Shui emphasised the influence and importance of compass directions and locations. Good or bad Feng Shui was defined in terms of the suitability of directions based on a person's date of birth, as well as on an investigation of the relevant elements influencing a person's life.

Compass Feng Shui also introduces the concept of time dimensions into Feng Shui, using the Lo Shu magic square to provide the basis of Numerology calculations. Compass Feng Shui thus addresses both spatial as well as time concepts of Feng Shi,

In contrast to the Form School, it assigned only minor importance to landscape configurations, and relied heavily on complex and mechanical calculations.

The premier name associated with the Form school was **Wang Chih** who came from Fukien province and lived during the Sung Dynasty. He too left behind a legacy of books which have been studied to this day, the most well known being the "Canon of the Core or Centre" and his "Disquisitions on the Queries and Answers" both of which were preserved and published by his disciple, Yeh Shui Liang.

By the late nineteenth and early twentieth centuries however the two schools had merged completely. Theories of the Form School including beliefs in Dragon symbolism gained wider acceptability and practice, although the principles of both schools have been analysed, discoursed upon and compared through the centuries.

Modern Feng Shui practitioners in Hong Kong and Taiwan customarily practise a hazy combination of both schools. Generally, the Form School with its heavy emphasis on the natural landscape requires a greater amount of intuitive insight. It is therefore considered harder to practice even though the *Green Dragon, White Tiger* symbolisms are relatively easy to comprehend. The Compass School method is harder to learn and understand, but once mastered is considered easier to practise due to its more precise methodologies.

CHI: THE COSMIC BREATH

Central to the Form School of Feng Shui is the concept of the vital Dragon's breath, the cosmic *chi*. Feng Shui, as practised today and through the centuries is all about capturing this vital *chi*.

Chi is the Energy, the life force that pervades Man's existence. *Chi* is created when a monk sits in meditation and breathes correctly; when a Kung Fu expert gives a well aimed blow; when the Master artist or calligrapher makes a brushstroke; *Chi* is also created in Nature, in the gentle meandering flow of water; or in the shape of a mountain.

The Cosmic *chi* of the *Green Dragon* is its breath, and it is where this valuable breath can be created and accumulated that great good fortune can be tapped. This Cosmic *chi* is the source of peace and prosperity, abundant wealth, honour and good health. In areas where this *chi* exists and accumulates, homes or abodes built there will benefit the household through several generations.

Chi is invisble. It travels through the atmosphere, unseen and without sound. Yet it exists and is very powerful. In the modern context, *chi* can be equated with the energy lines we now know move all round us. The environment is crowded with energy lines. What we call radio waves, satellite transmissions and so forth, the Chinse ancients call the *Dragon's cosmic breath* !

Feng Shui is all about capturing this breath which is favourable and auspicious. Thus *chi*, the dragon's breath, must not be scattered or blown away. If this happens there can be no good luck. In places where fast, strong winds blow, c*hi* is scattered and dispersed.

Usually "*chi* rides the winds and disperses". Unprotected windy sites are thus considered bad. When bounded by water however, c*hi* halts and accumulates. Thus places with the presence of water are usually auspicious locations.

Nevertheless, the kind of water must also be assessed because where there are fast flowing or straight rivers, these too, can carry the c*hi* away almost as soon as it is created. Places such as these are similarly to be avoided as all good luck will evaporate. At the same time c*hi* must also not be allowed to stagnate, or grow stale or tired. This too will causes all good luck to dissipate

One begins to understand now that the amount of c*hi* flowing, and whether it accumulates, stagnates or is rapidly dispersed at any particular location form the crux of landscape Feng Shui.

For a site to be auspicious, it must have access to or be near a good strong supply and flow of c*hi*. And because it comes from the *dragon*, places which house the *dragon* are said to offer excellent feng shui.

So where are dragons found ? The expertise of a Feng Shui Master lies in his ability to find the green *dragon*, and of course there are guidelines for doing this. But excellent *chi* flows are not necessarily all concentrated on the main vein or artery of the dragon's body. Other parts of the dragon also offer good healthy *chi* !

It should be clear by now that references to the *dragon* in a feng shui context therefore refer to the natural structures of the physical landscape - hills and mountain ranges, rivers and streams. In Feng Shui there are *land dragons* and *water dragons*. The Form School teaches us therefore how to look for these *dragons*, or failing that, how to create these *dragons* !

Having found the dragon, the essence of good Feng Shui practice is to trap the c*hi* energy released by the dragon. This *chi* will be flowing through the site, and we must then try to capture it, accumulate it without allowing it to go stagnant.

Where the Dragon's breath can be contained or where a permanent supply can be built up there will definitely be wealth and prosperity. Feng Shui guidelines thus focus on the methods that can be employed to harness the Dragon's breath.

 SHAR CHI

The accepted theory is that this will not be where there are straight vertical ridges or hills which instead send out killing breath which threaten and overcome the dragon's breath. This killing breath or *shar chi*, looks something like this sketch here. It is dangerous and hostile, bringing sickness and misfortune ! Unlike the good chi, *shar chi* travels in straight lines.

The concept of *chi* and understanding it is thus fundamental to the correct practice and application of Feng Shui.

 THE FIVE ELEMENTS

Feng Shui is also very much influenced by the theory of the Elements. In the Chinese scheme of the Universe, there are five of these elements, i.e. <u>Wood, Fire, Metal, Earth and Water</u>. All Chinese astrological sciences including the times, years and dates of birth are categorised as one of these elements.

The five elements are associated with colours, seasons, years, months, days, hours, seasons, and most relevant of all to the practice of Feng Shui, with compass directions. Once you understand which direction symbolises which element, and more, you understand which element destroys which other element; and which element produces which other element, you will have grasped a very vital aspect of in depth feng shui practice !

And in the process you would also have begun to understand a great deal about the other Chinese astrological sciences all of which interprets astrologicaol readings based on element analysis.

What are these elements ? Basically, the Chinese categorise everything in the Universe as being one of these elements, which are fire, water, metal, wood and earth.

FIRE is red, an auspicious colour. Fire is also summer, and is represented by the direction <u>South.</u> If you want to activate fire, think of anything red; think of the sun, think of bright lights and think of warmth and heat. Under the Chinese horoscope system, fire is also represented by the two animalsthe snake and the horse.

Fire destroys the element metal, and it also exhausts the element wood. In turn fire is destroyed by water. But fire produces earth and is thus exhausted by earth.

WATER is represented by the colour black. It is also Winter and is represented by the direction <u>North</u> If you wish to activate water, think of the colours black and blue; think also of fish tanks and aquariums, waterfalls and fountains, rivers and streams, drains and lakes ... Under the horoscope system of Chinese zodiac animals the two animals that represent water are the rat and the boar.

The element water destroys fire, and is in turn destroyed by earth. Water produces wood and is thus exhausted by wood; and it is produced by metal. Thus water exhausts metal.

WOOD is represented by all shades of the colour green, and its season is Spring. In Feng Shui, the direction <u>East</u> symbolises big wood and the direction <u>Southeast</u> symbolises small wood. If you want to simulate wood, think of plants and trees. Think of furniture and wooden pannellings. Think of paper and bamboo. And think also of the Zodiac animals, rabbit and tiger.

In the cycle of element relationships, wood produces fire and is thus exhausted by it. In turn it is produced by water and thus it exhausts water. The destructive cycle says wood is destroyed by metal, and in turn destroys earth.

METAL is represented by the colours white, silver and gold. Obviously any metallic colour also represents metal. Its season is autumn, and in the Pa Kua, its directions are <u>West</u>, which represent small metal, as well as <u>Northwest</u> which signifies big metal. In the Chinese Zodiac the animals, rooster and monkey represents metal. If you wish to activate metal, think of coins ! And think of money and gold bars. Think of jewellery. Think of electronic objects and cars, ships and aeroplanes ! Everything that can be mined is considered as metal.

In the cycle of relationships, metal is produced by earth and thus it exhausts earth. In turn metal produces water, thus exhausting water. Metal is also said to destroy wood and is in turn destroyed by fire.

EARTH is represented by all shades of brown, and while the earth colour is also yellow, very bright yellow sometimes also represents fire. The earth element is not representative of any season, Instead it is said to represent every third month of each of the four seasons.

In the Pa Kua, the earth directions are <u>Southwest</u> which represents big earth, and <u>Northeast</u> which is small earth, and also the centre. If you want activate earth think of all kinds of natural crystals, think of sand and silica. Think of bricks and cement and other building materials. Think of rocks and boulders. Think of the globe. Think also of the four animals of the Chinese Zodiac which represents the earth element. These are the ox, the dragon, the sheep and the dog.

And in the cycle of relationships, earth produces metal and is in turn produced by fire. Thus earth exhausts fire and is exhausted by metal. Earth also destroys water and is destroyed by wood.

The important thing to note about the elements is they have the mutually productive cycle and a mutually destructive cycles. Understanding this is central to element analysis for not just Feng Shui but also all the other Chinese astrological sciences.

In the <u>PRODUCTIVE CYCLE:</u>

Fire produces Earth,
Earth produces Metal
Metal produces Water
Water produces Wood
Wood produces Fire.

In the <u>DESTRUCTIVE CYCLE:</u>

Wood destroys Earth
Earth destroys Water
Water destroys Fire
Fire destroys Metal
Metal destroys Wood.

In considering the Feng Shui of locations and home interiors, understanding these two cycles of the elements allows the practitioner to incorporate his/her astrological element to be in harmony, and productive with the surrounding. Thus if you are born in a FIRE year, too much water in the home would not be beneficial (i.e. black coloured things, ponds, artificial waterfalls etc.) since Water destroys Fire. On the other hand, lots of plants or green things (Wood) and indeed a wooden house would be very auspicious because Wood produces Fire. Additionally it would be beneficial if one slept in the room located on the south side of the house or apartment.

Another example. If you were born in an EARTH year, and was of the earth element based on your animal year, then having too many plants (Wood) would not be very auspicious. On the other hand, having red things, lights etc. (Fire) would be very conducive since Fire produces earth. Earth people should sleep near or at the centre portion of the house.

YOUR ELEMENT
according to
TIME OF BIRTH

11pm-1am: WOOD. To face NORTH
1am-3am : WOOD. To face N.NE.
3am-5am : FIRE. To face E.NE.
5am-7am : FIRE. To face EAST.
7am-9am : EARTH. To face E.SE.
9am-11am: EARTH. To face S.SE.
11am-1pm: METAL. To face SOUTH.
1pm-3pm : METAL. To face S.SE.
3pm-5pm : WATER. To face W.SW.
5pm-7pm : WATER. To face WEST.
7pm-9pm : WATER. To face W.NW.
9pm-11pm: WATER. To face N.NW.

From these examples one can begin to see the various combinations that would work or not work from a Feng Shui point of view. Usually when the various members of the a family are born under different elements, then the Element of the Head of the Household should be considered for the main rooms and the entrance. All other individual rooms can be designed to benefit the main occupant of each individual room.

Meanwhile, you can further use the table on this page to check your Element according to your hour of birth. The relevant directions indicated for your Element can be used to orientate your Front Door, or to determine the best orientation for your office desk, or your sleeping position.

On the next page is a table that indicates the elements according to the year of birth (1900-1995). Use these tables to check the elements that determine your good fortune.

CHECK YOUR ELEMENT AGAINST YOUR YEAR OF BIRTH

* Years of the RAT:
    1900 Metal; 1912 Water; 1924 Wood; 1936 Fire
    1948 Earth; 1960 Metal; 1972 Water; 1984 Wood

* Years of the OX:
    1901 Metal; 1913 Water; 1925 Wood; 1937 Fire
    1949 Earth; 1961 Metal; 1973 Water; 1985 Wood

* Years of the TIGER:
    1902 Water;1914 Wood; 1926 Fire; 1938 Earth
    1950 Metal; 1962 Water; 1974 Wood; 1986 Fire

* Years of the RABBIT:
    1903 Water; 1915 Wood; 1927 Fire; 1939 Earth
    1951 Metal; 1963 Water; 1975 Wood; 1987 Fire

* Years of the DRAGON:
    1904 Wood; 1916 Fire; 1928 Earth; 1940 Metal
    1952 Water; 1964 Wood; 1976 Fire; 1988 Earth

* Years of the SNAKE:
    1905 Wood; 1917 Fire; 1929 Earth; 1941 Metal
    1953 Water; 1965 Wood; 1977 Fire; 1989 Earth

* Years of the HORSE:
    1906 Fire; 1918 Earth; 1930 Metal; 1942 Water
    1954 Wood; 1966 Fire; 1978 Earth; 1990 Metal

* Years of the SHEEP:
    1907 Fire; 1919 Earth; 1931 Metal; 1943 Water
    1955 Wood: 1967 Fire; 1979 Earth; 1991 Metal

* Years of the MONKEY:
    1907 Earth; 1920 Metal; 1932 Water; 1944 Wood
    1956 Fire; 1968 Earth; 1980 Metal; 1992 Water.

* Years of the ROOSTER:
    1908 Earth; 1921 Metal; 1933 Water; 1945 Wood
    1957 Fire; 1969 Earth; 1981 Metal; 1993 Water

* Years of the DOG:
    1909 Metal; 1922 Water; 1934 Wood; 1946 Fire
    1958 Earth; 1970 Metal; 1982 Water; 1994 Wood

* Years of the BOAR:
    1910 Metal; 1923 Water; 1935 Wood; 1947 Fire
    1959 Earth; 1971 Metal; 1983 Water; 1995 Wood

THE I CHING

The I Ching or Book of Changes is one of the most important books in the world's literature. Its origins go back to mythical antiquity and nearly all that is greatest and most significant in the five thousand years of Chinese cultural history and practice has either taken its inspiration from the I Ching, or has exerted an influence on the interpretation of its texts and meanings.

Both branches of Chinese philosophy, Confucianism and Taoism have their common roots in the I Ching. Indeed the philosophy, the sciences and the statecrafts, even the common everyday life of the Chinese are saturated with its influence.
What is the I Ching ?

It is China's most ancient text. It is the root of its civilisation. The I Ching is also the only Confucian Classic that escaped the Great Burning of Books that took place under the Emperor Chin Shih Huang Ti in 213 BC.

The I Ching is the source of all Chinese thought and practise. It stresses the fundamental connections between Man's destiny and nature, and provides an overview of the Universe as an entity, with all things in it being in constant flux, i.e. change. It was originally formulated over 4500 years ago by FU HSI, the legendary Chinese Ruler, who, in the words of Ernest Eitel *"looking upwards contemplated the images in the Heavens, and looking downwards observed the patterns on the Earth".*

Thus did Fu Hsi gain insights into the laws of nature and the influence of the cosmic forces on all life below. In his wisdom he instituted a practice resembling Feng Shui to sanctify the lives of his people, attune them to the moods and rhythms of Nature and provide them with a sense of continuity and security.

More than anything else, Feng Shui was influenced by the philosophy and text of the I Ching, suggesting that Man's destiny floats with the ebbs and flows of Nature's tides, and suggesting also that Nature's forces, as represented by the negative and positive, Yin and Yang, must exist in harmony.

Yin and Yang are primordial forces which are opposites.

THE YIN YANG SYMBOL

Yin is dark, Yang is light. Yin is passive, Yang is active.
Yin is female, Yang is male. But Yin and Yang are complementary, not opposing forces. Yin Yang is pictorially represented by the universally known symbol which depicts an egg showing the yolk and the white strongly differentiated, the black and white colours distinguishing the two principles.

YANG symbolises Heaven, the Sun, Light, Vigour, Positive Energy. Yang is the Dragon, Male, Strong, Hard, Fiery, Hot, Warm, Even numbers, Moving and Living. In Feng Shui, mountains and raised landforms represent Yang.

YIN symbolises the Earth, the Moon, Darkness, Female, and governs the Cold, the Soft, the Deadly, the Odd Numbers, the Negative. Yin is the Tiger in Feng Shui. Valleys and streams and water possess Yin qualities.

YIN and YANG together constitute the TAO, the Way, the eternal principle of heaven and earth: the Universe, whose life and breath is chi. Yin and Yang depend on each other, and give meaning to the existence of man. Thus without dark, there can be no light. Without hot, there is no cold. Without death there is no life. Without stillness there can be no movement.

YIN and YANG continually interact, creating change. Thus, Summer gives way to Winter which then gives way to Summer once more. Night follows day. The Moon gives way to the Sun. Darkness becomes Light. And so forth. Applying the Yin and Yang principle to Man, and man's fate, one is told that bad luck improves giving way to good fortune. And excellent fortunes can turn bad.

Man's fortune fluctuates, sometimes good, sometimes bad. This is referred to as the Tao of mankind and constitutes a cardinal principle of the text of the I Ching, the Book of Changes.

In Feng Shui, as with all things Chinese, the principle is that harmony must be maintained between these two forces. Too much Yang is no good. Neither is too much Yin.

For example, a completely flat landscape is said to be too Yin. There must be introduced to such a landscape some raised landforms which represent the Yang. Likewise, a completely hilly landscape with no rivers or plants cannot be balanced because it is too Yang. There must also be valleys and waterways to balance out the environment. And again, in any landscape, there must be shady sides and sunny sides, thus ensuring the Yin and Yang aspects of the Universe.

Hence gently undulating landscapes best represent the Yin Yang balance that is so crucial for there to be harmony in Nature.

This principle of balance is a cardinal rule of Feng Shui. Thus for example a completely flat compound can be balanced with shrubs, plants, ponds, boulders, trees. But if any of these are too large and overwhelms the garden or the house then there is disharmony, leading to bad Feng Shui. Residents will suffer the consequences of imbalance with regular sickness & bad luck.

Feng Shui requires that Yin and Yang must be in harmony, in balance and in equilibrium. And because both forces are in a constant state of flux, those who would wish to live with good Feng Shui orientation must be constantly alert to changes in the environment that affect this equilibrium, and thus adapt or correct accordingly, e.g. when a little tree grows into a big tree, its effects on one's fortune changes, as do the presence of boulders that change colour due to the rain and sun; and the shifts in the sun's rays as the year progress....or more to the point, when progress and development creates major massive changes to one's surrounding landscape. It is therefore important to be aware of changes, and to be alert to the effects of Change.

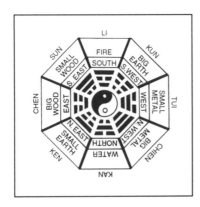

THE PA KUA

The Pa Kua is an octagonal shaped symbol that depicts the four cardinal points of the compass and the four subpoints. In accordance with the Chinese Compass the South is shown at the top, the North at the bottom, the East is on the left and the west on the right. The Pa Kua symbol derives its significance from the eight trigrams that are placed around its edges.

The Pa Kua shape plays a centrally powerful role in the practise of Feng Shui as it is one of the most important "cures" used by practitioners to ward off poison arrows or bad influences that represent a threat to homes or locations. Pa Kuas are also credited with having the power to ward off malevolent spirits. It is believed that the Eight Trigrams of the I Ching give the Pa Kua its potency and power.

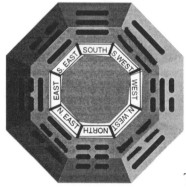

THE FORMER HEAVEN SEQUENCE

THE LATER HEAVEN SEQUENCE

The Trigrams are three tier combinations of Yin and Yang, broken and unbroken lines. Each of these Trigrams symbolise several things, and they are arranged around the Pa Kua in either the Former Heaven Sequence, or the Later Heaven Sequence. The history behind the two arrangements need not concern us but the fact that they are radically different is a significant point to note.

According to modern interpretations of the two arrangements, the Former Heaven Sequence represents the ideal version of the Universe as depicted by the Trigrams, while the Later Heaven Sequence represents the practical application of the Trigrams to the Earth, and by extension is strategically more important for the earth's *chi.*

The Later Heaven Sequence also corresponds with the Lo Shu diagram, which in its original version is actually the so called three by three *magic square*.

The arrangement of numbers 1 to 9 in the square are such that no matter which way the numbers are viewed each set of three numbers add up to 15, which coincides with the number of days in each of the 24 phases of the solar year. In this Later Heaven arrangement of the Trigrams, the Yin(odd) numbers form the cardinal points i.e., the numbers 9, 7, 1, and 3, with the remaining odd number, 5, in the centre. The Yang (even) numbers are the sub cardinal points.

4	9	2
3	5	7
8	1	6

THE LO SHU SQUARE

For Feng Shui purposes, the way to use the Later Heaven Sequence arrangement of the Trigrams is that one can superimpose the *magic square*, with its nine chambers onto one's home and from there, one can, by using the meanings of the Trigrams as an indication find out the best rooms of one's house for any specific member of the family. As each Trigram is associated with one or other member so he/she will benefit if his/herbedroom is located in this part of the house.

SUPERSTITION & SYMBOLISM

Feng Shui is closely connected to superstitious beliefs and the innate symbolism that is so much a characteristic of the Chinese, particularly rural Chinese. A mountain for example can be a fierce or benevolent dragon. An overhanging rock can be a Tiger's jaw. Or a malignant Frog. Or a fierce Eagle ready to pounce ! The natural environment takes on metaphorical qualities so that all manner and shapes of hills can be watchdogs, elephants, tigers or dragons; Rivers can also be dragons or serpents. And depending on the way and direction in which such "animals" are aligned to the dwelling place they may be good or bad, protective or threatening.

Often, rural folk and farmers, reared against a background of extreme superstition, can come up with extraordinarily creative interpretations of landforms. Hence a bad harvest may be due to the presence of a hill which resembles a rat; a successful and prosperous village may owe its prosperity to the presence of an exceptionally benevolent dragon; a town which produces lots of beautiful maidens may be due to the presence of the heavenly phoenix.....and so forth.

In Chinese folklore there are all sorts of superstitious beliefs surrounding the Dragon. In essence, Dragons are believed to bring wealth and prosperity when they are contented and appeased, as when the Sky Dragons bring the life giving rain that grow the crops and lead to a rich harvest.

Or they can wreak destruction and death by causing floods, earthquakes and typhoons when angry or aroused.

The Earth Dragons that live in the mountains generally associated with Feng Shui can also bring massive bad luck when any parts of their body or limbs are cut or wounded, caused by insensitive development and construction. It is for this reason that so many rural villagers of Hong Kong created so much fuss, and put up so many objections each time the Government implemented the building of roads, or tunnels or developments.

To understand Feng Shui, one needs a firm grasp of the basis of Chinese superstitious beliefs, many of which cannot be dismissed as mere old wives tales. Rather they provide the backdrop for many aspects of Feng Shui practice today.

3. APPLICATIONS OF FENG SHUI

In olden days Feng Shui was practised by the Emperors and the aristocratic class in China. Palaces and tombs; Stately Chinese homes were frequently built in strict accordance with Feng Shui principles. The Chinese ruling classes have always addressed a great deal of consideration and effort to the selection of gravesites for ancestors (generally referred to as YIN dwellings) as well as to homes for themselves (generally considered as YANG dwellings).
Historical records freely attest to this.

The design of the Ming Tombs on the Northwest outskirts of Beijing for example presents the best example of Feng Shui practice for gravesites, and demonstrates the overwhelming belief by China's Imperial family in the importance of Feng Shui.

The names of the hills surrounding the Ming Tombs reflect Feng Shui terminology. Thus the hills to the East are called the *Green Dragon Mountain* while those to the West are called the *White Tiger Hills*.

FENG SHUI FOR BURIAL GROUNDS

An important aspect of the Chinese Psyche has been the practise of ancestor worship and Feng Shui principles were usually very carefully applied when selecting sites for burials of ancestors. It was believed that ancestors were objects of veneration, and that if their final resting places were placed in good Feng Shui locations, then their descendants, for many generations would prosper and enjoy good fortune, their lives blessed with honour, fame, recognition, material wealth, long lives and plenty of male offsprings.

The fortunes of the living thus could even be *manipulated* to some extent by the favourable siting of the tombs of ancestors. This belief continues to be practised today, especially in Taiwan, where, on one of my visits I was told an interesting story of a highly successful and powerful family whose fortunes suddenly took a turn for the worse when an unscrupulous competitor desecrated the graves of that family's ancestors. Because of this possibility many wealthy families often purchase the land in front of their ancestors graves to guard against the construction of anything which may damage their Feng Shui.

The Chinese also believe that Sun Yat-Sen's outstanding success during the turn of the century was due to the extremely favourable position of his mother's grave in Clearwater Bay in the New Territories of Hong Kong, which exhibits all the classical requirements of a good Feng Shui location, complete with Dragon/Tiger configurations as well as a southern view of the waters of the South China Sea. Here in Hong Kong, careful attention continues to be accorded to ancestor burial sites, and cemeteries usually sit on excellent locations where lush greenery abound and views of the sea are available.

In the siting of graves Feng Shui men use many of the same principles as those applied to dwelling places for the living. They also recommend constant vigilance be paid to the maintenance of grave sites, and during the annual All Souls Day practised by the Chinese when descendants ascend to the mountains to pay their respects to their ancestors, the graves are usually cleaned and thoroughly checked. If the gravestone changes colour for instance, immediate steps must be taken to correct this. Thus a blackening of gravestones indicate the advent of disaster while the appearance of white usually portends a period of mourning for the family. The normal practice is to paint the red "jusha" medicine powder onto gravestones.

Graves are also supposed to be located on dry ground to prevent overly fast decomposition of bodies and coffins. Plots should also be regular shaped and facing the sea with a narrow inner portion and a wide entrance. Surrounding landscape should also be conducive to attracting *chi* so that descendants will all prosper.

FENG SHUI FOR TOWNS & CITIES

Feng Shui was also used in the design of towns and cities.

An excellent example is the favourable situation of the thriving southern city of Canton, which is located at the location formed by two ranges of hills gently curving and forming a complete horseshoe, a most favourable aspect. The chain of hills to the east of Canton, called the White Clouds represent the Green Dragon and the undulating hills on the other side of the Pearl River represent the White Tiger. Modern examples of Feng Shui oriented cities are not as well defined as in the classic example of Canton.

I have been told that the Feng Shui of Hong Kong is so good that despite the advent of 1997, Hong Kong will always prosper. This is because almost all buildings and roads are planned with Feng Shui considerations. My attention was also drawn to Victoria Harbour which resembles a *money bag*. Exits from the Harbour are small, thus allowing money to be held in. Excellent Feng Shui locations also abound in the Repulse Bay areas on the south side of the island where gentle undulating hills (indicating the presence of *dragons*) curve in horseshoe formations towards the sea. As matter of interest, I can personally attest to the fact that many of the Colony's most successful taipans and tycoons have their homes built on the south side of the island facing Repulse Bay.

Closer to home, in Malaysia, shortly after I returned in 1989, I played host to a friend from Hong Kong, who although not a Feng Shui master is extremely knowledgeable about the subject. We drove round the city of Kuala Lumpur at night and he made an interesting remark.

He said, *So many lights .... this is very good Feng Shui indeed.* Then again when he saw the trees and the rich foliage scattered around the city, once again he commented, *This is very good Feng Shui, you know...surely your country must be prospering.* And of course we are, but there will of course, be those who will tell us that a country's growth is due to other factors. Be that as it may, having good feng shui does help !

FENG SHUI FOR HOMES, DWELLINGS & OFFICES.

In recent years, Feng Shui has enjoyed a tremendous revival, and with the publishing of various treatises and books on the subject, the practise of Feng Shui is now well within reach of everyone.

Businessmen, especially those in Hong Kong, Singapore and Taiwan, and even in Malaysia, have been using Feng Shui guidelines when looking for suitable locations for their homes and office buildings. certainly the practice of Feng Shui is gaining increasing acceptance and respect among business people and used extensively in the design of commercial premises. The reasons are obvious. Many have seen Feng Shui cause havoc to business enterprises. It has also been observed to work for most of those who practise it seriously.

Feng Shui belief has also been extended to apartment and condominium living, to the interior design of rooms and offices, shopping malls and restaurants, housing estates and holiday resorts, hotels and head office buildings.

The booming business enjoyed by the increasingly expanding coterie of Feng Shui Masters and experts, especially in Hong Kong attest to its widespread practice. These masters have spent many years studying and practising it as a profession.

Modern applications of Feng Shui combine the precepts of both the Form School and the Compass School, so that not only are Dragon symbolisms used, but also compass directions and calculations based on birth dates are taken into account.

Generally the principle of harnessing the vital dragon's breath, the cosmic c*hi*, as well as the scrupulous avoidance of *poison arrows* i.e. Sha *Chi* are applied in the practise of modern Feng Shui. In cities, concrete buildings take the place of hills when trying to identify green dragons and white tigers. And man made roads, poles and eaves of roofs represent deadly poison arrows.

Another important component in the modern practise of Feng Shui is Water or *Shui*, which is often harnessed to lend additional value to the Feng Shui of buildings, homes and rooms. Water, in the Chinese scheme of things represent money and when properly sited, water brings great good fortune in the form of material wealth.

Trees, plants and boulders, because they represent Nature are also used to improve the Feng Shui of homes and buildings, as are Pa Kuas, flutes, lights, mirrors and crystals.

It is in Hong Kong that the practise of interior Feng Shui has been honed to a fine art, due mainly to necessity. A huge percentage of Hong Kong's population live in apartments and high rise buildings in this bustling concrete metropolis.

In assessing sites and locations it is important not merely to look for *good* Feng Shui characteristics. Equally vital, in fact perhaps more important, one needs to be on the lookout for and to beware of deadly poison arrows, which often come in the form of sharp angles and straight lines pointed directly at the entrance of buildings or homes.

Anything that can even be remotely construed as threatening, such as a rock which looks like a fierce animal, or a neighbour's antique cannon, a curved flyover which resembles a huge knife, or a large spire or cross, or even a tree that points at or blocks one's entrance should be avoided. Or they should be dealt with by installing Feng Shui *cures* that work by dissipating the effect of the *poison,* or by being blocked from view.

All this and more is Feng Shui. There is a great deal of common sense that needs to be applied to its practice. Plus a sensitivity to the importance of symbolism. Almost every object represents something to the Chinese mind, either because of phonetic similarity (e.g. the Chinese love the number 8 because it sounds like *growth)* or because of some quality the object possesses, or it may just be tradition.

The compilation of Feng Shui beliefs, principles, concepts, facts and suggestions contained in this book represents all that the writer has soaked up from practitioners and books. But the fundamentals of the underlying philosophies of serious Feng Shui have been extracted from old texts on the subject.

Would be practitioners are urged to use this book with sufficient consideration being given to the fundamentals and basic concepts.

Finally, a word of warning which was passed to me by every Feng Shui Master. It is a very ambitious person indeed who would offer to *check out* the Feng Shui of someone else's home or office. Studying the subject for personal use is one thing. It is useful and effective and really also very interesting. Practising it for others is something else.

Especially, practising it as a profession for material gain. This is because there is a great deal of experience and judgement involved in the practise of Feng Shui, judgements that really require serious commitment, experience, a great deal of meditative study, and an enormous amount of knowledge of the ancient classics of China, most of which are quite beyond the realm of the average person.

So do be careful.

The Phoenix sings in the Western Mountains,
Honour and Prosperity comes for 800 years.

PART TWO

4. THE BEST FENG SHUI LOCATIONS

GREEN DRAGON WHITE TIGER FORMATIONS

The classical method for detecting the best Feng Shui locations commences with the search for Dragons. In Feng Shui terms, the *Dragon* is a symbolic representation. The *Dragon* is epitomised by elevated land mass. The search for Dragons thus involve looking for ranges of hills and mountains that can resemble or symbolise the *Green Dragon* (Chinese texts also refer to the *Azure Dragon*). Usually where there is found the *true dragon*, there too will be found the *White Tiger*.

Dragons and *Tigers* are discovered by studying hill and mountain formations, by analysing the elevations of the ground, the colour of the foliage, and the contours of the surroundings. Level plains with no gradations of contours, or places with steep hills cannot symbolise *Dragons*.

The *Dragon* usually rests hidden in gently undulating hills and ridges. In practice they are not easy to locate. Hill formations do not offer clear indications of their presence, and different hill shapes exist side by side making the task an extremely difficult one. Pragmatic Masters in Hong Kong suggest some vital clues that can be followed.

My Feng Shui man, for example advise to search for secluded corners, where the vegetation is verdant, where there are gentle breezes and also where the air smells good. In such spots the elusive *Dragon* could indeed be hidden, closely intertwined with the *Tiger*.

Avoid the tops of hills for these are often unprotected places. Circumvent spots that have overhanging ridges or rocks for these are where malevolent *chi* accumulates. *Dragons* typically avoid such places. Bypass localities with bad air or which are damp and musty. Also avert hard rocky soil for it is *lifeless* and cannot represent the *Dragon*.

higher, more elevated than the *Tiger* hills. Where these two celestial creatures are present they are usually situated in such a way as to resemble an armchair, or a horseshoe. Thus the two ranges of hills will curve towards each other gracefully. When such a formation is present and the vegetation in the area looks lush and healthy, it is a sure indication of the presence of the true *Dragon*. Such places are very auspicious sites. An elaboration of the simple *Dragon Tiger* configuration which takes into account the directions of the compass involves also two other directions, i.e. North and South, and these are represented by the Black Tortoise (north) at the back, supporting the location ; and the vermilion Phoenix in the south, a small *footstool* type formation. When all four directions of the compass and animals are present, the symbolism is complete.

This sketch above attempts to demonstrate the perfect feng shui orientation. The precise spot of maximum chi creation is where the green dragon of the East is sexually interlocked in embrace with the white tiger of the West. In practical terms this describes an armchair formation of hills, where the west hills are rounder and lower than the east hills. In front there is a small little hillock (the red phoenix) for you to rest your feet, and at the back there is a range of hills (the black turtle) to give you support. If you build your house nestled as shown above, you are guaranteed to enjoy a life of great and meaningful abundance. In addition to material wealth and prosperity for many generations there will also be recognition, and the family will have a long line of distinguished descendants.

TRAPPING THE VITAL COSMIC BREATH

The objective of finding the Green Dragon and the White Tiger is to locate places where there is a maximum amount of "sheng Chi - the Dragon's Cosmic breath. This is the most vital element of Feng Shui, for it is this Chi, which brings auspicious good fortune.

Feng Shui masters and every book on the subject declare that the greatest accumulation of Chi occurs at the portion of the landscape where the loins of the Dragon and the Tiger are locked together in intercourse. The male (Yang) Dragon copulates with the female (Yin) Tiger to create generous quantities of Cosmic chi. Here then is created the harmonious balance of Yin and Yang. Thus the most ideal configuration has the Dragon on the left, the Tiger on the right and their extremities meet to form a perfect armchair. At the back is the Turtle and in front of them the Phoenix.

This formation is described in lyrical terms by the Manuals as The Dragon protecting pearl, and by others as the point where Yin and Yang meet in perfect Earthly Union.

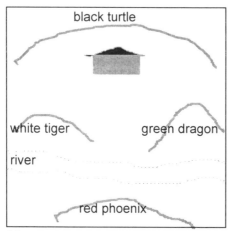

Families who build their homes on such locations are able to directly enjoy the Dragon's breath, thus benefiting from abundant good luck, good health and massive wealth for themselves and their descendants. There is of course only one point of sexual contact between the two ranges of hills coupling in the form of the Dragon and Tiger, obviously limiting the number of prime Feng Shui configurations.

However while the principal site is the most desirable, there are other tributary Chi locations which are also acceptable. Usually once the true undulating course of the Dragon is found, as traced in the outlines of hills it is also possible to identify the Dragon's head, his limbs, and even the veins and arteries of his great body. Thus the ridges and lines in the landscape form his body, veins and pulse. The streams and pools and underground water courses form his blood.

It is useful to know that different parts of the *Dragon's* body emit different degrees of cosmic c*hi*. Experienced Feng Shui practitioners are aware that there is an abundance of vigorous c*hi* near its heart and belly. The extremities of the *Dragons* body, such as his tail are, in contrast, areas of stagnant or tired c*hi*. Thus the Chinese warn against building one's home on the tail of the *dragon*, as this could lead to unsettling situations each time the *dragon* moved and swished its tail. A house on its head is equally risky, since one could come dangerously close to the *dragon's* mouth and be eaten up.

Localities where the cosmic breath is scattered by fast winds or carried away by fast flowing and straight rivers have no Feng Shui potential. Any good luck accumulated at the location will quickly evaporate. A site is only auspicious when it is near to, or on a place where a good strong flow of c*hi* collects and accumulates yet does not stagnate. Here is where the true *Dragon's* lair is located.

 How does one identify places where c*hi* may be scattered ?

The accepted guideline is that c*hi* cannot be built up when there are straight vertical ridges of hills. Waterways or rivers should not be fast flowing or straight. *Dragon* lairs must be near slow moving, meandering rivers and be protected against harsh winds.

Hill tops are generally not regarded as good Feng Shui locations. The scattering of c*hi* is so significant that even if one succeeds in locating the *armchair* formation, if there are harsh winds or sharp pointed hills in the area, the site is not considered auspicious.

Stephen Skinner, who has written one of the most comprehensive manuals on Feng Shui in recent years says in his book, *An ideal site is one protected from high winds by a northern screen of trees or hills, a place in which streams and rivers meander slowly, which nestles in the embrace of hills like an armchair, with a view facing south, all in a horse shoe shape*

Usually when a site is bounded by water, c*hi* halts and accumulates. When the site is unprotected from winds c*hi* is scattered. Here then are the two elements of Feng Shui; Wind and Water. The <u>wind</u>, if tamed to a gentle breeze will bring the circulating c*hi*; The <u>water</u>, if curved and nicely oriented will keep the c*hi* in the site, thereby improving its physical and spiritual fertility. The third factor is to ensure that the c*hi* does not stagnate.

If these things can be achieved by the natural configurations of the landscape, then an excellent *Dragon's* lair has been discovered. If the lair has the appropriate balance of Yin and Yang landforms, then the necessary energy exists to attract large quantities of *Chi.*

AVOIDING *SHA CHI*

Feng Shui repeatedly warn against *secret POISON arrows* which bring deadly killing c*hi,* generally referred to as Sha c*hi.*

These come in the form of straight lines, sharp angles or anything that is shaped this way, and generally includes straight hill ridges, vertical sloping hills, houses & buildings that have sharp angled roofs pointed at the site, railway embankments, straight rivers, roads, telegraph wires and any kind of straight or parallel lines that seem to be aimed directly and in a threatening way at the site, or at one's home, or even worse aimed at one's main front door. Straight lines bring bad luck, adverse fortune, disasters and sometimes even death.

Straight lines and angles are so dangerous that even in the ideal Green *Dragon*/White *Tiger* configurations, if there are ridges running in straight lines which point at the site, or any man made constructions that threaten the site in this way, it is a dangerous location which must be avoided. This is because the symbolic poison arrow would wound the *Dragon,* thereby creating massive quantities of poisonous c*hi.*

Be wary of this deadly sha c*hi.* Guard against this evil breath which is caused by the disharmony created by pointed symbols, straight lines and sharp angles. It is because of this principle that all Feng Shui Masters agree that one must strenuously avoid locations facing a straight road, as in T-junctions. And also why they tell us that main doors must never face angles created by the roof lines of neighbouring buildings. All these situations create bad c*hi* and can hurt family and business fortunes.

If it is not possible to do anything about poison arrows that are already aimed at one's home however, Feng Shui offers some practical remedies.

Bearing in mind that the practice of Feng Shui subscribes to the principle that it is what one sees that makes the difference, all variations of poison arrows can be screened off by growing trees with thick foliage. This disperses killing *chi* with great efficiency, especially if the leaves of the tree are broad.

SHAN: SHAPES OF MOUNTAINS & HILLS

To the *Chi*nese mind, mountains have always been desirable places of abode. This is explained by the deep seated conviction that celestial *Dragons* nestle in elevated landforms. Flat plains hold no allure as these exemplify tired discarded droppings washed down from the mountains. Not surprisingly then that mountains epitomise the practise of Feng Shui.

The practitioner however must be able to differentiate between the different shapes of mountains and hills, and to grasp what each of these configurations portray in terms of the Five Elements, and in terms of their influence. It is also critical to be able to recognise which shapes are compatible, and which are not.

Hills and mountains can be classified into five main shapes according to their structure and profile when viewed from the horizon. These take into account the shape of their summits, and their angles of steepness.

From the descriptions here, the seasoned practitioner can draw some judgements of compatibility with each of the mountain shape by comparing the Element of the mountain with his own Element based on his year of birth. Similarly using his information of the productive and destructive cycles of the Elements he can also judge whether he is compatible with the mountain.

There are basically five types of mountains, Conical, Round, Square, Oblong and Ridged. These are fully described with sketches on the next page.

CONICAL: The peak rises up sharp, bold and straight, rising to a keenly edged sharp point. This mountain type is identified with the planet MARS, and represents the Element FIRE. People born under the Element Metal should not live on this type of mountain. Those born in the Years of the Element Earth however would benefit from living on this kind of conical shaped hillside. Be wary however if this kind of mountain faces your home, since they are generally purveyors of malignant *chi*.

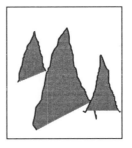

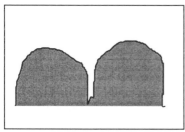

ROUND: The mountain or hill rises straight has a long body, but rounds up at the summit. Such a mountain is relatively narrow. This Shan is identified with the planet Jupiter, and represents the element Wood.People born in the years of the element fire are especially suited to this kind of mountain residence, while those born in the earth element years are advised to avoid this kind of mountain shape.

SQUARE: The mountain looks more like a plateau with a flat extensive summit.This mountain is Saturn, and represents the element Earth. Square shaped mountains are ideal for those born in the years of the metal element but are unsuitable for those born in water years.

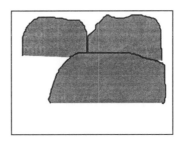

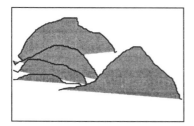

OBLONG: The mountain looks softly rounded, has a broader base and gentle slopes. This Shan is identified with Venus, and represents the Element Metal. Oblong shaped hills are suitable for those born during water years, and not suitable for those born in wood years.

RIDGED : The mountain appears to have several summits; it seems alive and undulating and looks like a continuos range. This type is identified with the planet Mercury, and the element represented is Water. Ridged shaped mountains are good for those born during the years of the wood element but not suitable for those born in fire years.

 SHUI
WATERWAYS, RIVERS & PONDS

In Feng shui, water represents wealth and money. Water is a crucial element in the practice because they are the most obvious lines of flow of the cosmic *chi*. To understand and appreciate the significance of a waterway, be it river, stream, canal or drain, it is important to remember that in general anything that is fast flowing and gushes in a straight line is not good, while anything that meanders and flows gently is preferred. Thus straight waterways are usually unacceptable as a feng shui feature, since *chi* gets conducted away, rather than towards the site.

Slow meandering, winding and deep water courses are very favorable for collecting and accumulating *chi*, especially if they form a pool or a pond in front of the site, home or building. The principle as always is that water must be balanced, neither too fast nor too slow as to be non moving or stagnant.

Students of water feng shui refer to the WATER DRAGON CLASSIC for insights into the feng shui treatment of water and waterways. This specialized manual which describes the formation of water *chi* was written around 600AD.

The Classic contains many drawings and diagrams that show different variations of waterway formations, expounding on the good and undesirable configurations, locations and direction of flows. The diagrams offer detailed interpretations of the symbolic use of elements, compass directions and other constellations. For the purposes of this book it is necessary only to extract some examples to demonstrate general guidelines from the Manual

> ❂ For those keen on going deep into water feng shui, you can refer to my book devoted exclusively to he subject entitled WATER FENG SHUI FOR WEALTH. This book contains the complete water *chi* formulas

The *chi* referred to in the WATER DRAGON CLASSIC is identified by the shape of watercourses. From the water which flows on the surface in streams and rivers, lakes and pools, *chi* are said to ascend into he skies even as water evaporates.

Wind then distributes the water vapor as clouds which take the form of sky *chi* in the air. Clouds bring the life giving rain to mountains and the earth below, and the cycle is complete. Water feng shui taps into he energy or life giving forces of this cycle o divert valuable *chi* into one's home.

House facing a curving river. Excellent feng shui

Reproduced on these pages are diagrams from the Manual showing natural river formations and desirable feng shui sites. From these drawings, one can take note that the Classic recommends that the home should be built at the site which represents the belly of the *chi*. The Manual classifies watercourse into trunks and branches, and generally suggests that homes should best be built amongst the branches i.e. the tributaries of rivers. It must be surrounded by and nestle protected by the water branches.

These tributaries and streams usually feed the main river and the more branch tributaries there are, the more potent will be the accumulation of *chi*. And the reason for not being too near the main river itself is because here in the mainstream water flows too fast, thereby preventing the gentle penetration of *chi* into a house or building.

Generally, curved and winding rivers offer better potential for locating good feng shui sites. It follow therefore that the best indications of *chi* concentrations must also be where two branch streams or rivers meet at a junction. The meeting point however should not be sharp but instead should curve or bend gracefully.

In water feng shui, the Form School is vitally important in the sense that the shape and form of the waterway must be assessed according to Form School guidelines. The water feng shui formulas however are based on accurate readings of he feng shui compass.

Some of the general guidelines pertaining to water are:

* Yin and Yang balance must be maintained. Thus landscaping is
  important, and there must be combinations of sunlight and shade.
* Water should be shielded from poison arrows. Use trees to *achieve* this.
* Shapes, if artificially created must curve and bend, and not be sharp.
* Water must never be allowed to stagnate or grow foul and stale.

Always maintain harmony with nature, let the dimensions blend in with
the surroundings so that the waterways created are neither too big nor
too small. Proportions must achieve yin/yang balance. There are also
other variations to the use of water related objects utilized to enhance
feng shui.   In Hong Kong, particularly, residents freely resort to
introducing aquariums, little fountains and artificial waterfalls to enhance
the feng shui of their businesses and homes

*Residents of a house sited next to a beautiful waterfall provided the waterfall
does not overwhelm the house, will enjoy great wealth for many generations !*

MAN MADE ADJUSTMENTS TO THE LANDSCAPE

When the natural contours of the landscape are lacking, or where there is an insufficient balance of the forces or elements, thus bringing disharmony to a location, Feng Shui advocates that thoughtful altering of the landscape is advisable e.g. the effect of straight rivers and hills that threaten life, money and prosperity can and should be modified by growing clumps of trees that provide protection and shelter.

Sometimes altering the land; building a road, installing a pool, digging through the mountain to build tunnels, cutting down of trees, constructing buildings - all these man made adjustments to the land almost always disrupts the currents and flow of c*hi*. Sometimes the Green *Dragon* can also be injured and wounded by excavations.

Feng Shui suggests that in assessing a site one must therefore look for, and be conscious of the presence of existing or potential *development oriented* changes that may be made to the landscape thereby affecting the Feng Shui of the area. Thus for instance, digging through hills and mountains to construct tunnels and build straight roads cannot be good, because straight roads bring Sha c*hi* and *poison arrows*. Roads and construction work can also upset the balance of Yin and Yang, the flow of c*hi*, and the currents of wind and water. Or worst still injure the *Dragon*.

In olden China, when the emperor Shih Huang Ti ordered the building of the great wall, the feng shui of the country was believed to have been affected drastically ... and indeed millions of China's men died at the wall ! Since thne of course the wall has come to symbolise a structure of great sorrow for the Chinese, and there are any number of heartwrenching legends and stories all filled with tears and heartbreak associated with the wall.

Sometimes changes to the landscape are only temporary, as when modern day property developers clear entire ranges of hills to make way for rows of terrace houses, shophouses and in recent years, for condominiums. Barren of trees, the red earth exposed and looking suspiciously like wounded *Dragon* flesh, these are scenes that could scare off any Feng Shui conscious, would-be buyer.

And yet, after the housing estate has been developed and residents move in, trees are once more planted, lovely landscaping with shrubs and flowers and even artificial pools, the place begins to look balanced and attractive once again.

A very good example of this phenomena is BANGSAR, probably one of the most auspicious neighbourhoods in suburban Kuala Lumpur - indeed everyone who lives here has prospered ! Probably this area houses one of the most prosperous gathering of residents in the city, with many of today's successful businessmen starting out life in this area. Yet when the place was first developed the barren looking hills provided little indication of its future prosperity.

In today's world where the pace of development is moving so fast, and when hills get cut and forests get cleared with unseeming haste, these changes, which often take place in neighbouring suburbs will definitely have an impact on the feng shui of the jouses and buildings nearby.

Happily in feng shui conscious societies/countries, much is also done to temper the massive changes to the landscape with attractive and auspicious landscaping. Thus in places like Singapore and Malaysia, many of the massive yang like structures are softened with huge doses of yin features, Trees continue to be grown even on city streets; artificial waterways are built. Old mining pools get a new lease of life with attractive planting and landscaping. In these instances, progress has improved rather than spoilt the feng shui of the place.

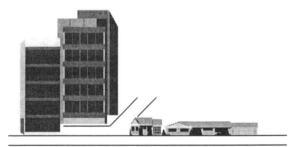

At a personal level, however, you must always watch out for massive new buildings, new roads, flyovers, power stations, transmission lines and other similar large structures which could create some problems for you. Huge new buildings built next to your tiny house will surely create imbalance and you must take corrective measures accordingly.

PART THREE
5. FENG SHUI FOR CITY DWELLERS

TOWNHOUSES & BUNGALOWS

In towns and cities the natural landscape - hills, mountains, vegetation, and water - have been affected or replaced with roads, high rise edifices and all kinds of man made structures. The shapes and dimensions of buildings, drains, flyovers, sewerage pipes and other construction often mean that the practice of Feng Shui must confront a totally new kind of environment that differs sharply from those that had been in existence when the practice was first formulated.

Modern practitioners need to adapt traditional principles in an intelligent, logical and sensitive manner, to present day circumstances. Because of the subjectivity involved in the practice of modern city type Feng Shui, there are variations in the way Feng Shui rules are explained and interpreted. Viewed from this perspective one can understand the sometimes apparently conflicting opinions and judgements of Feng Shui experts. In spite of this, if one applies a sensitive appreciation of underlying Feng Shui concepts when assessing potential locations for one's home in the city, one will not go far wrong.

For urban and city dwellers who live in townhouses, bungalows and linkhomes, Feng Shui rules, principles and influences discussed in the first two chapters must continue to be considered e.g. the search for places with good *Chi*, the balancing of Yin and Yang, and the natural harmonious balanced living with Nature. And the matching of the environment with one's relevant element. Plus an eye for the superstitious backdrop against which all Feng Shui is practised. These continue to be the basic guidelines to follow. Simultaneously one must also beware of poison arrows and Sha *Chi* caused by a very long list of objects, both natural and man made which can precipitate inauspicious consequences. Thus the first step in practising feng shui is to become familiar with the underlying philosphy and concepts upon which the science is based. Incidentally it is perhaps relevant to point out that I do not subscribe to the intuitive approach in the practice of feng shui. Common sense yes, because much of feng shui recommendations make good sound common sense, but it is not an *intuitive art* ! Implement the recommendations correctly and you WILL enjoy feng shui. It CAN be learnt !

6. CONSIDERATION OF LOCATIONS

All cities and towns have heavy traffic built up centres and suburban locations. In looking for a good Feng Shui location or in assessing a plot of land earmarked for one's personal dwelling place, firstly determine the Feng Shui qualities of the general surroundings of the plot of land being considered.

If it is in the suburbs, near hilly or undulating land, first try to look for possible green dragon white tiger formations. Study the shapes and dimensions of elevated landforms. Look also for waterways, rivers, mining pools or other natural bodies of water. In doing this, at all times take account of man made constructions and include these in your overall assessment of locations.

If the land being appraised is in the City centre, use creative imagery and develop an awareness for details. Neighbouring buildings, their shapes, size, colour and other characteristics can represent dragons and tigers, tortoises and phoenixes. Use directions and building heights as clues. In city centres look also at the roads. Are they straight and threatening ? Are they nicely curved ? Are there clock towers, flagpoles, church spires nearby that can upset the flow of *Chi* into your piece of land ?

If there are different levels to roads nearby, examine their contours and see whether roads are leading downwards or upwards towards you. Do the roads have gentle or sharp gradients ?

Is your land located at a junction of two, three or four roads? Are any of the roads pointed straight at you ? Are there trees planted in the neighbouring streets ? Are there rivers, large drains or bodies of water nearby ? Be on the lookout for structures that might be threatening, or pointed directly at the location. And. always look out for *poison arrows*

Develop a keen awareness of the things to look out for .... things like Straight Roads, Transmission Towers, Sharp Roof Lines, Concree water tanks, Sharp Corners of Buildings....that point directly at your land. These could be Poison arrows.........

The shape of elevated landforms (hills) and buildings are crucial in town Feng Shui. These offer abundant imagery normally associated with rural areas; dragons, tigers, phoenixes, tortoises and the rest.

THINGS TO WATCH OUT FOR:

If you have a choice these are some of the structures you want to try to avoid. Try not to have your home built too near these structures, and definitely, they should not be pointing directly at your main front door. These structures are generally referred to as poison arrows which bring *killing breath* or shar *chi.*

A church steeple , especially if pointed directly at your door is inauspicious. There will be too much yin energy directed towards you.

Transmission or other towers generate bad *chi.* Avoid building your home near sites which are near or adjacent to these structures.

Try not to live too near power stations or factories which have tall towers like these, They create inauspicious *chi.*

Avoid being at the end or junction of a straight road, especially if the traffic seems to be heading towards your home. This is one of the most serious manifestations of *poison arrows* and should be avoided.

Remember that anything which seems threatening or hostile is best avoided. And always try to steer clear of structures that are pointed or angled. Structures like these are usually bad news ! The most common indication of an angled poison arrow are pointed roof lines of neighbouring buildings. Like this roof line shown here.

Flat featureless land generally offer unexciting potential for good Feng Shui. They may not be bad, i.e. they may not bring misfortune, but they do not offer good auspicious luck either ! Thus if the housing estate or township you are investigating to buy a new a home has rows and rows of linkhouses, all of the same height on totally flat land, the external landscape does not promise much in terms of Feng Shui. Gently undulating land presents better possibilities. Only this type of landscape has the possibility of housing the auspicious green dragon !

At the same time, places on hillsides which are subjected to strong harsh winds are usually bad Feng Shui. In these places *chi* cannot accumulate, as they are rapidly blown away as soon as they are created. Thus unprotected places hold little promise of good fortune.

LOCATIONS TO AVOID

AVOID HILLTOPS
Generally, traditional Feng Shui tells us to AVOID locating homes at the very top of hills, especially where such locations are not sheltered from winds by natural clumps of trees. Hilltops are also places where water tends to flow away, thus scattering vital *Chi*.
However where such sites have a higher range of mountains nearby which seem to give it some *"protection"*, then the site takes on a different configuration. In such a case just make sure the dwelling place is not sited in a way which has its front door facing the protective hill. Remember to always have the hills behind your house. This provides support and shelter, and shields you from bad *chi*.

AVOID PLACES WITH
THE POTENTIAL OF *POISON ARROWS*.
Avoid any location where threatening natural or manmade objects point at a dwelling built there, bringing *poison arrows*.

We have seen that this can be a straight road, or it can be caused by a straight ridge of hills caused by a neighbouring mountain range. It can also be caused by massive transmission and other towers, or sharp knifelike angles caused by nearby houses, condominiums or buildings. Or even a disproportionately tall or massive structure facing your land, which could affect your front door or entrance.

Shown here are more examples of "*poison arrows*.
Do not forget the powerful influence of symbolism and imagery.
While the more obvious offenders are straight roads, sharp corners and angled roof lines, sometimes a structure opposite may in fact generate malignant *chi* just because it resembles a fierce animal or symbolise a weapon. *Poison arrows* are especially deadly if they are directly pointed at front doors and entrance ways.

If you face a big hill as shown above the indication is that the feng shui is most inauspicious. Try installing a light pole to dissipate the bad chi caused by the hill !

If your front door faces a single big tree, it is very harmful. Cut the tree down !

Do note however, that trees behind the home are considered to afford protection for the house, as they symbolise something to lean on. Trees in front of the home are acceptable if they are a distance away. The worst offenders are trees that have a single tree trunk, like pine trees, casuarina tress, coconut trees and the like ! For years my husband and I could not conceive a child because there was a single casuarina tree just ten metres in front of my main door. In those days neither my husband nor I knew very much about feng shui and it was only after we moved into my present home (which was built according to good feng shui) that we had our daughter !

*The edge of a flyover
hitting this townhouse
is really bad news indeed!
Unfortunately there is
very little to be done*

Sometimes, due to changes in roadworks, or when a new highway gets built near where you live, your feng shui can get altered in a negative way because of massive concrete flyovers. If and when this happens, there is very little really that can be done. This is because such structures are usually so massive that nothing you put up in defence can deflect the huge amount of shar *chi* created !

In Hong Kong during the late Eighties, a very prominent businessman was strenuously warned by his feng shui master to move out of his home because a huge new flyover was *cutting into the belly* of his home. He was too busy to make the arrangements and as a result, the man got into trouble, was arrested by the Anti-corruption agency and subsequenlty endured two years of great stress. He also very nearly went to jail ! After he moved out of his home however, he eventually successfully resolved all his legal problems.

Sharp edge causes poison arrow

The edge of this huge building symbolises a most dangerous *poison arrow*. If your house entrance faces such a sharp edge, the consequences will be very bad indeed. Ill fortune comes in the form of loss financially, a great deal of illness and someimes even fatal accidents can occur. To deal with this sort of *poison arrow*, you really will have to judge the strength of the shar *chi* coming your way. The bigger the building the more deadly the shar *chi* ! Usually the best solution is to move out, but if you cannot, then try using a cannon to deflect the shar *chi*. Use this method only as a last resort.

AVOID PLACES WITH OVERHANGING CLIFFS
Land plots that are located at sites with overhanging cliffs or large landforms further up can be interpreted as threatening Tigers Jaws or Frogs that are poised to pounce. Such places can be highly dangerous.

The most famous story of a Feng Shui type tragedy occurred in Hong Kong during the Seventies when a luxury apartment block located halfway up the island at Mid Levels collapsed, killing hundreds of residents. Feng Shui men had repeatedly warned that an overhanging cliff that resembled a <u>frog</u> was poised quite threateningly above the apartment block. And indeed there were those who were fortunate enough to take heed of the warning and moved out thereby saving themselves when the block collapsed during a particularly bad rainstorm.

In Feng Shui, anything resembling the frog and appearing to threaten the home must be dealt with.

In old Chinese feng shui books there are stories that relate the effect of rocks and large boulders which resemble the deadly frog. One tale has it that a great famine occurred in a village because that season's harvests were destroyed. Village elders blamed the misfortune which had befallen the village on a large boulder that overlooked the village. The boulder, they said resembled a pesky frog which had eaten up all the harvest ! Naturally when the boulder was removed, all became well.

AVOID PLACES WHERE VEGETATION LOOKS STARVED
Usually areas of good Feng Shui contain fertile soil, have sufficient water and sunlight, and good drainage that promote lush vegetation. When surrounding plants look weak and brown; when trees and vegetation betray a lack of green, such areas have bad feng shui.

Usually close examination of the gardens of homes already built in the area, or the trees planted on the streets or roads nearby, give sufficient clues. Prosperous housing estates or residential areas usually have gardens that are lush and verdant. Also avoid land which could have decayed tree stumps below. Survey the land before building on it. The dead stump causes ill health.

Dead or decaying trees indicate that the good chi flows in the area is lacking. Avoid building on such land.

AVOID AREAS WITH POOR DRAINAGE
Good Feng Shui sites usually have good drainage, and any waterways nearby should contain water that is clean and flowing, and preferably meandering. Monsoon drains which clog up with uncollected foul smelling garbage or are polluted with harmful chemicals conduct bad *Chi.* Thus unless something can be done to *"shut out"* such waterways from view, avoid such locations.

SHAPES & DIMENSIONS OF LAND PLOTS
Having evaluated the overall landscape of the location under consideration, next examine the plot of land being considered. In urban areas and cities where land values have shot up to dizzying heights in recent years, land plots for the building of houses are usually not large. They also often come in various shapes and dimensions. Sometimes, due to poor planning or subdivision, residential land can be lopsided in terms of dimensions.

Generally, for Feng Shui purposes, the perfectly square or rectangle shaped land are the best to work with because such shapes are easy shapes within which to design homes with good Feng Shui dimensions and considerations.

GOOD SHAPES: Squares & rectangles

Triangular shaped land is generally considered difficult to build on since special Feng Shui *"remedies"* have to be considered when designing the home. The same is also true for other shapes. When confronted with unusually shaped pieces of land, one generally requires the help of a Feng Shui master to advise on the house design.

UNFAVOURABLE SHAPES: Triangles, Incomplete, L shapes, U shaped

GRADIENTS

Land on which to build one's home should preferably be undulating, although flat land is also acceptable. But when gradients get too steep, especially if the land plot is small it is not favourable.

If there is a gradient, the house should be built such that the back of the house is higher than the front, thereby giving some kind of protection to the house. *Chi* will also flow from the back gently down the gradient to the front of the house. However please note that too steep a gradient will cause *Chi* to flow out of the household.

At the same time neither the backyard nor the front garden of the house should be disproportionately large or small as this will affect the fortunes of the household. At all times <u>balanced dimensions</u> should be maintained. When this rule is not observed the consequences can sometimes be a continuing spate of bad luck caused by imbalance.

Siting the house should also be done such that it gets a fair amount of sunlight. Generally the Chinese like to site their homes facing south as this allows the sun's rays to enter and warm the house. The preference for a south facing front door has its roots in the geography of *Chi*na where the South represents the source of warmth and the North represents the source of harsh cold winds.

Feng Shui Masters who subscribe to the Compass School hold the view that the preferred directions of a house, and its front door, should ideally be based on the year of birth of the Head of the household, as prescribed in books based on Wang Chi's ancient Manuals.

I have reproduced the complete formula for investigating each individual's auspicious and inauspicious directions in my second book on APPLIED PA KUA LO SHU FENG SHUI. These formulas, based on each person's date of birth offer excellent application guidelines on how to go about tapping one's most favourable directions.

For those yet unable to get their hands on my second book, but who wish nevertheless to follow some proper guidelines on orientations and compass directions, I reproduce here an alternative Table containing the preferred directions given in the YANG DWELLING CLASSIC. You can orientate your rooms accordingly.

DIRECTIONS ACCORDING TO
THE YANG DWELLING CLASSIC

✪ The most important rooms in the house should face SOUTH
✪ The main door should face SOUTH
✪ Kitchens should face EAST, and never SOUTHWEST
✪ Shops and Business premises should face SOUTH
✪ Commercial stores must never face NORTHEAST or SOUTHWEST
✪ Elder members of a family should face SOUTHEAST

BUILDING ON ODDSHAPED LAND.
As we have noted, land can come in many different shapes that are less than ideal. When one does not have the luxury of having a regular shaped plot of land, the best method of dealing with it from a Feng Shui point of view is to use one's imagination to design the house such that it activates the abode (land and house together) into a vital organism which can create or attract *chi.*

To do this first look at the land from all angles, its dimensions, gradients, bends, curves etc. Secondly see if it can resemble any kind of auspicious animal or creature or object.

Then applying concepts of balance and harmony you can begin to find creative and workable solutions. For example, garden fountains and lights can balance out gradients and disproportionate dimensions. The objective is either to *make* the land plot as regular shaped and balanced as possible by using lamp posts to demarcate artificial boundaries; or to make the land resemble some auspicious animal (e.g. a red bat or a dragon). The latter solution is not so easy since it is so dependant on judgemental inputs that require a great deal of experience. As such, I prefer to stick to the more conventional way, which is to make use of *lights* that create points of demarcation. These then symbolises extra land that serve to regularise its shape !

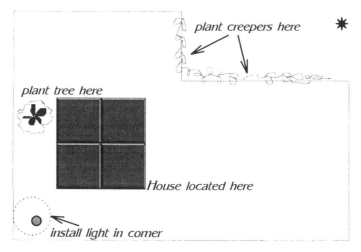

The above example show an L shaped piece of land. In this example creeper plants and a light pole have been used to compensate for the missing corner caused by the L shape of the land. Alternative soltion is to install a light pole at the spot marked with a ✳ . As this is outside the land it may not be so easy to arrange !

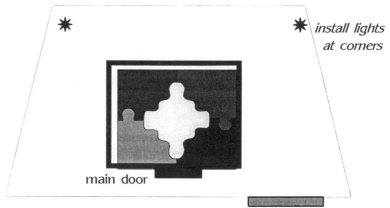

Irregular shaped land (above) made to seem regular with the use of two lights at corners at the back of the house !

In both of the preceding two examples, lights have been used to "*regularise*" the shape of the land. It is also possible to use boulders or create little ponds within the compound to simulate the presence of dragons. This creates favourable *chi* flows and can also often overcome the problem of irregular shaped land.

HARNESSING THE EARTH'S *CHI*

A prominent Feng Shui master in Hong Kong once offered me two methods of artificially harnessing the Earth's *Chi* to benefit a household. I reproduce these methods here for you to try;

To tap into the *Chi* which lies deep inside the earth, one can sink a hollow pole (copper or concrete pipe) into the ground from one's garden, then attach a light at the top of the pole. This will have the effect of attracting a good flow of *Chi* into one's compound thus benefiting one's luck and fortune.

Where one lives in a house which is suspected of suffering from stale or stagnant *Chi*, e.g. when plants do not grow, or the grass perpetually looks brown and barren, or when everything seems to be going wrong, try introducing objects which can generate good *Chi* and cause it to circulate favourably through the house. This can be done by installing lots of bright lights; or installing a miniature fountain or keeping a bubbling fishtank, or even installing musicalwindchimes at the tops of doorways.

THE FENG SHUI EFFECT OF ROADS

Flyovers & road interchanges should be viewed with extreme caution. Look at gradients and check if straight or sharp curves are pointed in the direction of your home. If so it is advisable to install Feng Shui cures.

In (a) these shophouses are *embraced* by a flyover. Planting a row of trees will camouflage the bad luck.

In (b) two rows of linkhouses face a straight road at the T junction, but the offending road is not directly facing the front door of the house units . No adverse effects are produced.

In (c) the road interchange resembles a cross and is harmful to residents nearby. Planting a cluster of trees to block the view of the interchange shields residents from adverse luck.

7. THE FENG SHUI HOUSE.

The manifold factors that have to be considered in building a house that can be said to have *good* Feng Shui can be summarised in terms of the various features to examine. A house with *good* feng shui is defined in several different ways. At the risk of making it sound too simplistic, we can say that as long as a house attracts good fortune to its residents, it has *good* feng shui.

However, feng shui itself can be viewed from several perspectives. Thus a house or apartment block, or an apartment or even just a room, can be said to have *good* feng shui for EVERYONE living in there !

OR it can be said that the feng shui is good only for people whose directions and room layouts coincide with the auspicious directions indicated by the date of birth of the residents.

OR it can be further qualified to mean that the auspicious feng shui occurs only during certain periods according to how specially calculated feng shui stars *fly* !

In short, the definitions of a *good* feng shui house depend very much on the School of Feng Shui practised; or the method of feng shui used! In this book, the attributes of a *good* feng shui house are defined mainly in terms of the FORM SCHOOL in which the physical structures in, and around the home are considered and analysed.

To a very large extent these physical structures are so basic to feng shui that if they are NOT correctly aligned, OR if there are structures that destroy the house's feng shui, then all the formulas in the world will be of no use. This is because physical *poison arrows* always have the potency to destroy *good* feng shui arranged or calculated under other methods. It is for this reason that this first introductory book focuses mainly, almost exclusively to taking care of the physical surroundings that affect feng shui !

After the practitioner has mastered these basics, (or at least, have created an awareness of what to be wary of) they can then proceed to study the more advanced formulas that address specific methods for activating or attracting specific types of *good* feng shui !

And then. even when they practice the more advanced feng shui, they will then be able to ensure that at all times, their homes, offices and rooms are never hit by the debilitating effects of the killing breath caused by *poison arrows*, and by yin/yang imbalances.

DRIVEWAYS:

The approach to a house should always be subtle and friendly, not direct and threatening. Thus Driveways should never come straight and rigid towards a house. A straight driveway especially, should not be pointed directly at the front or main door.

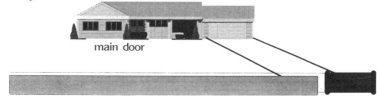

main door

*This straight driveway is NOT hitting at the main door
and is therefore not harmful*

The diagram above shows an example of an unfavourable driveway. It is straight and can be threatening. Fortunately however, notice that the main front door does not face the driveway. Instead it is at a right angle to it. As such the driveway does not threaten the house.

Feng Shui prescribes circular driveways or if this is not possible some kind of curved or meandering approach. Straight Driveways can however be softened with landscaping plants, bushes or flowering plants which break up and camouflage the sharpness and harshness of straight lines.

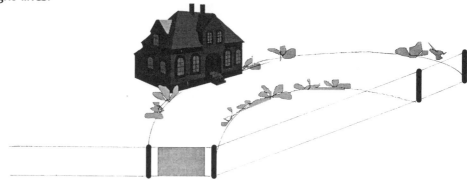

This curved driveway (above) is both pleasing and auspicious It is an example of a very favourable driveway. It is circular and thus promotes the smooth flow of *chi* into the house.

Driveways should not slope downwards away from the house. This causes *chi* to flow outwards, thus draining away money and good luck. Driveways that are either too narrow or which are disproportionately broad are also not auspicious. The guideline to follow is to design a driveway which blends with the dimensions of the house.

Driveways that are narrower than the main door are inauspicious. A driveway which narrows outwards is also bad, and is said to have a limiting effect on business and financial opportunities. Such a driveway is also bad for careers. The way to deal with this problem is to install lights at the narrow ends. This will supposedly mitigate the bad feng shui caused. See the sketch below. The driveway narrows outwards, but this has been dealt with by the installation of lights at the narrow ends. The driveway itself however is nice and broad so the residents will have good *chi*. At any rate do not have narrow driveways as these are inauspicious.

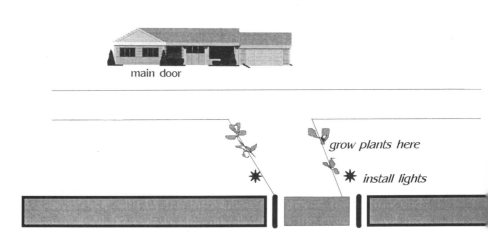

main door

grow plants here

install lights

Driveways can often be enhanced with shrubs abd flowering plants that have the capability to convey vital *chi* into homes. Usually the more healthy looking and colourful the plants are, the better will be the *chi* created. At any rate healthy planst in a garden (no matter how samll the garden) are always indicators of good feng shui !

DEADENDS :
Houses should preferably not be located at the end of *dead end* roads.. This type of location promotes the conduit of killing Sha *chi.* There is another reason. The Chinese believe that living in a dead end, one is *trapped* in, and should there be problems, there will *be no way out.* Problems, instead of getting better will get worse. And there can be no good luck to assist residents during times of difficulties.

NEIGHBOURING HOUSES:
The houses all round one's home affect one's Feng Shui, and especially the house that is situated directly in front of one's house.

Danger comes mainly from large roof angles that are pointed at one's front door.

Anything sharp, or angled or appears threatening (like an antique cannon or a huge pillar, a chimney, or even a large tree with a long big trunk) that is pointed at one's home is bad. These bring terrible bad luck and should be strenuously blocked from view if possible.

THREATENING OBJECTS INCLUDE THINGS LIKE:

An antique Cannon.

This is almost the ultimate *killing* symbol. Cannons, especially when they are antique and has thus *tasted blood* can be quite deadly if one just happens to be facing your entrance. They bring illness, financial loss as well as loss of opportunites. In downtown Kuala Lumpur, one of the main buildings in the Golden Triangle has been negatively affected by just such a cannon !

I also know of a woman, well versed in the science of feng shui who displays antique cannons outside her home. Her cannons have inadvertently wreaked havoc on some of her neighbours, probably without her intending them to be that way.

Thus when you investigate your feng shui, do keep a look out for something like this. Incidentally, the cannon is also a very powerful and potent tool to use if you need to deflect the *killing chi* of *poison arrows* threatening your home. Having said this however I strongly urge you not to use it unless there is nothing else you can do.

Anything pointed, sharp or crossed shape.

These can be roof lines, escalators or other decorative structures used by your neighbours to enhance the design of their homes/buildings. Look out especially for anything that is, or seems to be directly pointed at your home and its main door ! They are quite deadly !

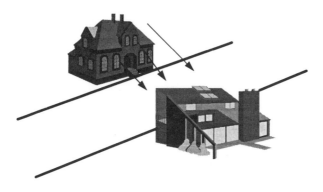

In this example above here, the bungalow house across the road has a roof line which forms a sharp pointed triangle that is directly threatening its neighbour across the road. If there is a similiar house like that facing your house, either plant a clump of trees to block off the poison arrow created by the roof line, or hang a large round mirror to reflect away the offending structure. In such situations, the Chinese often hang a Pa Kua mirror, although usually the small mirror of the Pa Kua is seldom strong enough to deflect the *killing chi*!

Sometimes even the colour of a neighbour's house or its shape can cause it to resemble a hostile creature or animal poised for attack at one's home. These are all deadly *arrows* and must be dealt with either with a Pa Kua mirror or by planting a tree with heavy foliage to block off the offending object thereby dispersing the killing *chi* before it reaches one's home.

TREES, a great antidote for poison arrows !
Use heavy foliage trees and large bushes to block out, or deflect the effect of poison arrows. They are very effective, these trees ! But make sure they have lots of foliage, are healthy and are planted as a clump rather than singly !

THE APPROACH ROAD

Feng Shui Masters strongly warn against having one's home face a road coming straight at one's front door. This happens if the house is located at a T junction as shown here.

The classical T junction !
A most inauspicious situation.

At nights, headlights that resemble fierce tigers aim their ferocity at the house. The fatal effect of this circumstance is deadly and bad health, strange accidents and even death faces households living in such homes. To verify this, just drive into any housing village, and look for houses whose front doors directly face a straight road aimed at them. You will find that these homes often look *sick*. Plants there do not flourish and the house itself just looks bad and very unhealthy.

GARDENS

In keeping with Feng Shui's central theme of maintaining balance and harmony, gardens can often be landscaped to artificially create good Feng Shui configurations. This can be done by creating elevated hillocks, flowing streams, rock waterfalls and planting lush vegetation. By ensuring that there is a good balance of Yin and Yang with the use of boulders, ponds, plants of various colours, the Feng Shui of homes can be enhanced. At all times be sure to maintain balance and harmony by keeping watch over size and dimensions. e.g. too large a pond or a hillock that is out of proportion to the garden or the house will do more harm than good. This is because the *chi* generated by, say, an artificial pond that is too large, will overwhelm the residents of the house, bringing setbacks into their lives.

Flowering plants, inside or outside the home are always good feng shui !

FENCES & WALLS

These serve to delineate the boundaries of the house from external influences. Walls, for instance are effective dividers which can block out the effect of harmful objects like boulders, fast flowing or clogged up drains, telephone poles and so forth. The design of walls should however be harmonised with the landscape.

Brick walls should have plants and foliage planted near it to create Yin Yang balance as shown in the diagram above. Fences made with wrought iron, or wood should not be designed with spikes or arrows pointing downwards (for this suggests going down) or with spikes pointed inwards, for these symbolise arrows pointing and attacking the house. If pointed upwards, as shown here below, the effect is nuetral. AT any rate do plant some shrubs near the fence.

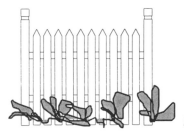

Wooden fences like this one here are acceptable

Chain link fences are also acceptable. Again plant
some shrubs or creepers nearby to create good yin and yang balance..

COURTYARDS: Feng Shui masters recommend that there be some kind of interior courtyard designed into a house. This may be an entrance courtyard, an interior court or even just an opening or chimney. The effect is to have an *opening* to the open air and attract good luck c*hi* into the house, and let its good effects permeate through the rooms in the house. having a courtyard also encourages *chi* to flow smoothly thereby generating happiness for the household and its residents. Nevertheless, this is not a very practical idea for modern type homes, unless you are wealthy enough to afford having this luxury.

HOUSE SHAPES

The best shapes are regular, i.e. square or rectangular. Round shapes are acceptable although this is seldom advisable as it presents layout problems when considering Feng Shui for interiors. Any of the almost infinite number of odd or irregular shapes can be the source of troublesome problems unless corrected.

If we consider just two of the unfavourable house shapes, the L shape and the U shape, both these shapes suggest *something missing*. Generally L shaped homes create business and money problems for residents while U shaped houses cause marital discord between spouses.

Feng Shui remedies can be in the form of lights installed at the *missing corner* of the L shaped house, or the installing of a mirror wall in the missing corner. For the U shaped house, the solution is to *cover up* the centre portion of the house and install two lights.

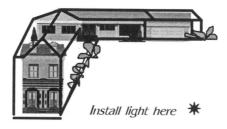

Install light here ✳

An L shaped house

MAIN DOOR :Even the most excellent Feng Shui of a house can be destroyed if the Main Door is oriented badly such that it is being attacked by deadly *poison arrows*, or its shape and size are not in Yin Yang harmony with the rest of the house. Usually if the main door has Feng Shui defects, extreme bad luck will befall the residents.

Well situated main doors as a rule, open into wide, bright rooms or lobbies and generate happy, expansive and comfortable feelings. Main doors should open into and have maximum view of house interiors. There should not be anything that can block the *chi* coming into the house through the Main door.

Entry for instance into a dark or narrow lobby area stifles the flow of c*hi* and is bad. This is usually corrected by installing a large mirror on one wall, and improving the lighting in the lobby area.

The main Door should also not open into a lobby of low ceiling, or where there are low heavy beams. This often causes illness to the inmates of the house. Again installing overhead lights can alleviate the problem to some extent. The subject of doors is dealt with in greater detail and with more illustrations in the section on Interiors, when we discuss Feng Shui for apartment living.

INTERIOR DOORS

The *Chi*nese do not like to have three or more doors, opening in a straight line, especially if one of these is the main door and one is the back door, as they believe that this results in *chi* coming in and then flowing straight out again, thus preventing the household from enjoying any good luck.

There are several Feng Shui remedies for the problem of three doors. One is to hang wind *chi*mes from the tops of the doors. Another solution is to place a screen in front of one of the doors thereby encouraging the *Chi* to flow round the screen instead of directly through the doors.

Doors should be regular shaped and not slanted. Otherwise extreme bad luck will be the result.

Doors leading to different rooms within the house should face each other directly and squarely, and they should be of the same size. Otherwise there will be family quarrels. There should also not be too many doors too close together for the same reason.

Finally doors that are seldom used, usually referred to as *dead* doors can also cause quarrels, and inhibit the flow of *chi*. To cure the problem of doors, Feng Shui suggests the use of mirrors which when installed on a door gives it depth thereby encouraging the flow of *chi*. Mirrors can also be used to align two facing doors which are not facing each other directly. Curtains or a pretty picture can be used to camouflage a door with sharp slant or doors which are irregular shaped.

WINDOWS

Correct placement of and dimensions of windows can affect the Feng Shui of a house. Windows should generally be regular shaped, and open completely, preferably outwards. This brings in the good luck chi and opens up opportunities for the residents of the household. Inward opening windows are generally considered harmful to careers, and money making opportunities will be lacking.

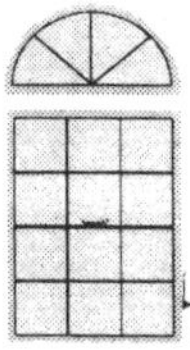

The Chinese do not like windows that slide up or downwards, nor windows that look into offensive views like a pole, a tree trunk or a sharp object.

Other offensive views which can cause bad luck to occur are church spires or crosses, the roof angles of a neighbouring house, a straight road, or a flyover that appears to be headed for the window.

Glare from the afternoon sun, or headlights from cars are also considered malignant. In such cases Feng Shui recommends closing the window with the offending view completely.

If there are too many windows in a house, this causes discord between parents and children. In such instances hanging windchimes or crystals will cure the problem.

BEAMS

As far as possible overhead beams should not be exposed. Nor should they be too low. Beams, when exposed hurt the chi of a family and are an obstacle to growth and wealth accumulation.

The modern day practise of having fancy plaster ceilings that have *dropped* beams, or worse, those with sharp angled designs at the corners are not good Feng Shui at all.

Beams (shown in the diagram on the next page) generally bring oppressive *Chi*, and when chairs, beds or desks are placed below an exposed beam, they cause headaches, bad luck and problems in business. Beams generally breed distrust and dishonesty.

Overhead beams can be dealt with in several ways.

Hang a windchime to disperse the bad chi, or hang two flutes, each tied with a red thread and have them angled as shown in the diagram here. Thia is actually the Pa Kua shape which is believed to more potent than windchimes, and are hence more effective.

While these remedies do work to relieve headaches and stress, generally, you would be well advise NOt to either sleep, or work directly beneath an exposed beam. This problem of overhead beams is actually more acute in offices, since they can often cause you to have quite a fair bit of

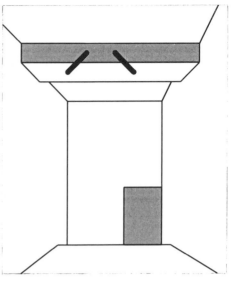

Overhead beam corrected with flutes

problems with both your subordiantes and with your boss.

So if you see a beam above you, do try to rearrange your desk or bed and get out of its way !

PROTRUDING CORNER COLUMNS

are also bad as beams, since these create sharp angles that hit out at the residents of the house. To remedy the problem of corner columns use plants to camouflage the sharp protruding knife like corners. This is shown in the sketch here.

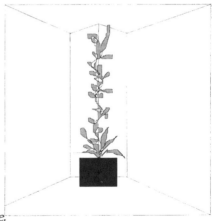

Use creeping plants to nullify the effect of protruding corners inside the house.

TOILETS

The Chinese are very particular about the placement and design of toilets and washrooms. Usually toilets should not be easily seen, and washrooms must not face important rooms like dining rooms or offices directly. For the more conservative, toilet placements are carefully calculated so that they do not occupy areas in the home which correspond to auspicious directions for the owners, and definitely toilets must not face front doors since this means that all the good *chi* which comes in will be in danger of being *flushed* away.

STAIRS

These should preferably be broad, rounded, and curved gracefully into a large hall. Spiral staircases are deadly especially when situated in the centre of the house, as it represents a corkscrew. Staircases should not start directly from the front door, as this allows the household's c*hi* to flow right out of the door.

The steps of the staircase should be solid and not have *holes* as is the case in so many mass constructed terrace houses. This causes money to flow out. The banisters should also not have sharp angles. They should be rounded and smooth. If there are any designs that resemble arrows these should be changed to something less threatening. Or at least should face upwards.

Finally staircases should be brightly lit as this conducts good c*hi* to the sleeping quarters. If the ceiling of the staircase is too low, thus oppressing the c*hi* flow, install a mirror on the ceiling and then fix a bright light to *lift* the ceiling.

 LIGHTS

As a general rule a house should be designed to be bright and airy, not dark and gloomy. Dark rooms and halls cause c*hi* to stagnate. Lights bring a strong dose of YANG into a house, especially during the Night time (YIN) hours. Feng Shui masters in Hong Kong strongly recommend the use of brightly lighted chandeliers for those who can afford it. This is because Chandeliers combine crystals with light and are therefore a wonderfully potent way of activating c*hi* within the house and causing it to circulate.

USE OF MIRRORS

Mirrors are generally used to *double up* good things in a house. because of this they are usually recommended for dining rooms where mirrored walls double up the food laid out on the eating table. Mirrors are also used to reflect into the house a pleasant exterior scene like a view of water (money) or a view of plants and flowers that bring nature into the home. Mirrors also reflect light thereby brightening homes and creating conducive environments and enhancing the c*hi* flow of a household. Finally mirrors enlarge the size of rooms thereby creating a feeling of space that is also conducive to the flow of c*hi*.

Mirrors when used, should preferably be high enough to reflect the people living in the home without *cutting off* their heads. Mirrors should also not be hung to reflect toilets (in bathrooms) or doors, especially the main door. Mirrors on the ceilings of studies and offices are supposed to be good since it represents reaching upwards.

USE OF PLANTS

Feng Shui widely prescribes the use of plants and flowers to uplift and expand the flow of c*hi*. Plants are excellent counter measures against any kind of sharp edges found around the house that may be caused by protruding columns, corners, angles of tables or other pieces of furniture.

Artificial plants are also acceptable provided these do not look *dead* or dried up, or allowed to get dirty with layers of dust or cobwebs. Plants represent life and nature and for it to generate c*hi* they must look healthy and verdant.

USE OF WATER:

The Chinese believe that introducing water into homes or offices almost always *draws* money in, the same way delightful scenes of lakes, rivers or seas reflected onto homes do. Often, Feng Shui masters advocate the use of wall mirrors to attract such views into the interiors of homes or apartments.

This belief in the potency of water lie behind the Chinese fondness for aquariums in which beautiful fish of all kinds are cared for, and the

water is kept gently bubbling with oxygen.
Aquariums are believed to generate healthy doses of c*hi*, especially when the water is clean and the fish are kept healthy. Chinese in Hong Kong have a preference for keeping goldfish and generally nine goldfish are kept, of which one must be black. This allows the single black one to absorb any bad c*hi* that may flow into the home, and its death is often interpreted as a misfortune absorbed or averted. In Malaysia the graceful Arrowana Fish is preferred as this fish is said to bring money,

DOWNWARD FACING ARROWS
and
SHARP ROOF ANGLES

The downward facing arrows placed on the facades of these link houses may be aesthetically attractive. From a Feng Shui view point however these *arrows* create Sha *chi* and could well symbolise failing fortunes. Indeed anything that suggests a downward movement is not auspicious. If your home has these designs it is advisable to paint these arrows white thereby *rubbing* them out.

Note also that the sharp pointed angle, i.e. the ⌃ formed by the roof lines is a deadly *poison arrow* aimed outwards. Please make certain that your link house, and

These Roof Angles are common examples of poison arrows......

Make sure such roofs do not point at your home and front door.

especially your front door does NOT face just such an angled roof from the link house opposite yours. If it does, instal a Pa Kua. When purchasing a linkhouse in any of the new housing estates, you would be well advised to request to see the designs of houses that will be built across from the house you are planning on purchasing.

LAYOUT OF ROOMS:

The layout of rooms within the home together with their dimensions, levels and general condition influence the attraction and circulation of c*hi.* To start with homes that are properly maintained, clean and *humming* efficiently, where the lights work, where drainage works, where plumbing works and where paints are not peeling, drains are not clogged, and doors and windows are not stuck, attract good c*hi.*

This is because such homes symbolise a healthy and happy environment. Residents of such homes often enjoy good health and do not succumb easily to illnesses or epidemics.

Feng Shui normally favour house layouts which have regular shaped rooms, and where individual rooms are not disproportionately large or are too small, unless dictated by the need and function of the rooms.

Ceilings should not be too high to the extent that residents get a *cramped* feeling of discomfort or feel overawed by soaring ceiling heights that are out of proportion to the size of the house.

The main door should open to a small lobby but should at the same time have a good view of the home interior. Living rooms or reception rooms where guests are entertained should be sufficiently large and welcoming to encourage the flow of c*hi.* Because the living room is the principal room associated with visitors it should never be higher in level to either the dining room or the kitchen. If it is, all the good c*hi* of the residents will attach themselves to *outsiders* instead of to residents.

Kitchens should ideally be situated on the right side of the house or next to the dining room where the family eats. If the kitchen is sited too far away, the family tends to have disagreements especially between c*hi*ldren and parents. Kitchens should be airy and clean as this is the place where all food is cooked, and c*hi* must be allowed to circulate gently, not stagnate.

Dining Rooms should not be too small, and round tables are preferred to rectangular tables. If possible the food on the dining table should be reflected in a mirror on one wall so that food is *doubled* up, symbolising plenty for the family. The Dining room is also the place to hang paintings of fruits or other kinds or good food to symbolise the continual availability of food for the family.

All bathrooms and toilets within a house must be located such that they do not face directly onto an opposite door, or worst still face the front door. The toilet bowl itself is where the wealth of a family or its good luck can be flushed away; thus toilets must never be at the end of a long corridor, or be easily visible from outside the toilet room.

Badly sited toilets or toilets which constantly clog up affect the health of the household. Feng Shui recommends that doors leading into bathrooms & toilets be kept closed at all times.

Bedrooms should ideally not be located in a row along a long corridor. This results in there being too many doors causing quarrels and disharmony. Besides long corridors are seldom encouraged as anything long and straight creates bad chi or fast flowing chi, both of which are anathema to good Feng Shui.

Ideally, the layout of rooms within a house must promote the good smooth flow of chi, and because chi moves in a graceful meandering fashion, flowing from room to room, the general layout of homes must be conducive for this. Openings and entrances, from one room to the next, should avoid being designed in straight lines.

LAYOUT ACCORDING TO THE PA KUA

A popular method of determining room layouts is to superimpose the Pa Kua octagonal shape onto a house, and plan the location of rooms in accordance with the directions and symbolism represented by the 8 Trigrams of the Pa Kua. The diagram shown here illustrates the Pa Kua with its eight Trigrams. A Trigram is a three tier combination of Yin and Yang lines, and each of the Trigrams is attributed to a point on the Compass.

SOUTH

The Pa Kua Shape

Pa Kuas hung up for Feng Shui purposes usually have the trigrams arranged according to the "Former Heaven Sequence", where Chien is placed South, K'un is North, Li is East and K'an is West. This arrangement supposedly depicts *the ideal* of the Universe.

There is also a second arrangement of the Trigrams which was developed later, and this came to be known as the "Later Heaven Arrangement".

This latter arrangement of the Trigrams puts Li in the South, K'an in the North, Chen in the East and Tui in the West. It came to be regarded as a more practical application of the Trigrams to the earth situation, i.e. it was a less idealised view of the world and was, accordingly more applicable. In using the Pa Kua to determine room layouts Feng Shui Masters almost universally prefer to use this more popular Later Heaven Arrangement of the Trigrams.

To apply this method for your room arrangements, examine the links detailed herewith below which matches each of the 8 Trigrams with their corresponding directions, as well as with the symbols and other associations yoi can use in your feng shui practic.e.

Next locate the position of the Main Door, then superimpose the Pa Kua onto your house plan. Follow on from there, using the representations and meanings of the Trigrams, summarised here. For further insights into this method you can refer to the I Ching (The Book of Changes) which offers more detailed interpretations and symbolism of the Trigrams. Just remember that the matching of the Trigrams with room layouts demonstrate qualities (attributed to each of the Trigrams) which are associated with chi entry and exit points at the eight main compass directions.

THE TRIGRAMS:

* CHIEN,
three unbroken lines, Yang, placed Northwest in the arrangement, is associated with the Head of the household, the male paternal, or patriarch. It also represents Heaven, the sky, the celestial sphere, strength, activity, power, bright colours, energy and perseverance. Thus in the northwest corner or sector of your house, it is useful to locate a room where th head of the household uses, or where he can work like a study or a main bedroom.

* KUN
three broken lines, yin, placed Southwest in the arrangement, representing the female maternal, earth, docility, dark colours ... In the SW part of the house place the mother figure.

* CHEN
two broken yin lines above an unbroken yang line, represents Spring; is placed East in the arrangement, and is generally associated with the eldest son. This trigram symbolises decision making, vehemence and shock. The eldest son's bedroom can be located in the East.

* SUN

two unbroken yang lines above a broken yin line, is placed <u>Southeast</u> in the arrangement and repesents the eldest daughter, wood, wind, and whiteness, Locate the eldest girl in the southwest part of the house.

* KAN

an unbroken yang line between two broken yin lines, placed <u>North</u> in the arrangement and representing winter, water, hidden things. Also represents the middle son. Locate him in the North corner of the house.

* LI

a broken yin line between two unbroken yang lines, is placed <u>South</u> in the arrangement and represents summer. The trigram symbolises beauty, brightness and fire. It represents the middle daughter, and her bedroom is best located in the south.

* KEN

an unbroken Yang line above two broken Yin lines, is placed <u>Northeast</u> in the arrangement and it represents the youngest son of the family. This part of the house is suitable for the youngest male person living in the residence.

* TUI

a broken yin line above two unbroken yang lines is placed <u>West</u> in the arrangement. It represents Autumn, joy, happiness and also, the youngest daughter. Tui also symbolises pleasure or a concubine as well as spiritual matters. Thus the room of the youngest girl in the residence should be located in the western part of the home. This location is also suitable for the family altar or family room.

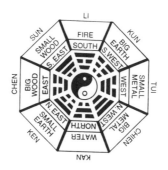

8. THE EIGHT LIFE SITUATIONS OF THE PA KUA

There is another popular approach to designing auspicious Feng Shui Layouts. This is also based on the Eight sided Pa Kua shape, and it divides each of the *corners* or directions of any house or room into "Eight Life Situations", the sum total of which universally represents the combined aspirations of mankind.

Each corner is believed to focus on one of these situations, and according to Feng Shui it is possible to *activate* any of these life situations to benefit residents.

The eight life situations are
Marriage, Fame, Wealth, Family,
Knowledge, Career, Mentors, and Children.

These life situations are located within every house, business premise, apartment or office. And they can be enhanced for the benefit of the resident. How is this done ?

First, by determining which part of the house (or room) represents each of the life situations.

There are two methods to do this.

* The first method uses the Directions to identify the Eight corresponding life situations with the Eight Trigrams based on the Later Heaven Arrangement of the Trigrams. It is then necessary to determine which of the Life Situations correspond to each of the

Eight Trigrams. This is summarised in the Box shown below.

THE LIFE SITUATIONS & CORRESPONDING TRIGRAM

CHIEN: Northwest governs the MENTORS or helpful people Sector
KUN: Southwest governs the MARRIAGE Sector
CHEN: East governs the FAMILY and health sector
SUN: Southeast governs the WEALTH or prosperity sector
K'AN: North governs the CAREER or opportunities sector
LI: South governs the FAME and Reputation sector
KEN: Northeast governs the Knowledge or study sector
TUI: West governs the CHILDREN sector

Determine which life situation you wish to activate. It can be any sector. Having decided on what you want, proceed to energise the relevant corner using various methods. I have dealt with these *"methods"* in some detail in Part 6, under the heading "Interiors." These methods include using any one of the several Feng Shui enhancing objects, like placing an extra bright light in the appropriate corner, hanging a windchime there, or installing a fish tank....

EXAMPLE: If you wish to *stimulate* the Wealth corner of your house, which according to the Pa Kua's Later Heaven Sequence is the corner represented by the Trigram, Sun (or the south-eastern part of the house), then this is the corner which must be activated. Pay special attention to the southeast side of your house. Place your study, your bedroom and your office in the southeast corner; and if you like, make sure there is always a Feng Shui *"enhancer"* placed in that corner. You can use plants, crystals, fountains, windchimes and so forth but my favourite for the southeast corner is to use a fresh and healthy looking plant ! This is because the southeast is represented by the element wood, and plants belong to the wood element. It is not necessary to overdo it though. Just one object is sufficient.

If for some reason the Wealth sector which you wish to activate is *missing* i.e. the Southeast corner is lacking, due perhaps to the shape of your house in the first place, you should try to *build in* this corner, i'e. Expand by extending your home. Or, failing this, use a wall mirror to *extend* the house into this corner. Alternatively place a light in the missing corner, outside the house.

For those who wish to use the Pa Kua to determine house shapes and layout arrangements, always superimpose the Pa Kua onto house plans before building.. The Pa Kua can be *"widened"* or *"stretched"* to ascertain the significant corners.

The second method of locating the relevant life situations in the home is by superimposing the same Pa Kua with the same code as above onto the whole house (or room) but in a FIXED way, totally ignoring the cardinal points or directions of the compass. This method identifies the areas corresponding to the different life situations after "FIXING" the Pa Kua with the <u>Trigram KAN parallel to the main door.</u>

Beautiful birds are delighted to fly from their cages,
Now the sky is the limit.

PART FOUR

9. FENG SHUI FOR APARTMENT DWELLERS

Modern day urban living entails coping with concrete landscapes which have been shaped by Man in his continuing quest for development. Those living in high rise apartments, condominiums or flats, who wish to practise Feng Shui to ensure their living ambience is conducive to a prosperous and happy existence, must adapt the traditional Feng Shui guidelines when planning or evaluating their apartments.

In doing this, it is useful to understand for example, that roads and highways can be likened to rivers and that Buildings and other man made structures can be likened to mountains. The overriding principle of harmony, as well as the cardinal requirement of maintaining Yin Yang balance continue to be significant and important rules to follow.

High rise buildings on one's left and right can also represent the Tiger and the Dragon, and views of water, and backward protecting hills are similarly favourable indications.

In attempting to understand the practice of Feng Shui in a modern day environment, use a certain amount of imagination and imagery. Dragons and Tigers and the cosmic *chi* can and do exist, thrive or stagnate in contemporary metropolises around the world.

Thus if you are an apartment dweller, perhaps even more so if you are, Feng Shui can work its *"geomantic magic"* if you make the effort to live in harmony with the natural Universe.

ASSESSING EXTERNAL LOCATIONS

When considering the purchase or rental of a condominium/apartment, focus first on the surrounding landscape and location of the entire development. Use the same guidelines contained in the earlier chapters, by carefully checking the surrounding hills or other high rise buildings nearby. See if their orientations are conducive or threatening.

Massive structures nearby that overshadow the building you are considering, especially if they are oriented to face the entrance are unsatisfactory and must be avoided.

Angled rooflines, sharply curving flyovers, straight roads or even worse, the sharp corners of neighbouring structures pointed at the entrance of the apartment block, all have malignant consequences.

In evaluating this aspect of Feng Shui, always use the main entrance of the apartment block, even though the particular apartment you are considering may have its main front door oriented differently from the main entrance of the entire building.

This is because the Feng Shui of the whole building must be evaluated before even examining the interior Feng Shui of the apartment itself.

Also examine the different levels of the surrounding landscape, and avoid buildings which have, or are built on sharply steep inclines, especially when the driveway leading to the apartment block slopes downwards, thus draining away all the good luck.

At the same time there should, ideally not be any roads located at levels that are midway up the apartment block as would be the case if the apartment building is built against a hillside.

Next look at the drainage of the development. Make sure that if there are any large monsoon drains, these are either covered or if not, that their orientation do not offer any threats, as it would do if these drains flow past the front entrance in full view. During heavy downpours such drains can get filled up with fierce fast flowing water which just sweeps away all the good *chi.* Many of the monsoon drains that presently exist in the Pantai and Damansara areas of Kuala Lumpur, and parts of Petaling Jaya in Malaysia, become raging waterways when there are heavy downpours. Do beware of these types of waterways.

Also check whether there are nearby mining pools or natural rivers. If so then depending on the way the apartment building is oriented, there is the potential for great good luck in living in such apartment blocks. Use the guidelines on Water to assess this aspect of the building's Feng Shui.

The orientations of the building must also be designed such that each of the apartments contained therein get combinations of sunlight and shade.

The landscape at the back of the building should ideally be slightly higher than the building itself.

In recent years there are a growing number of Real Estate developers, aided by their Architects and Engineers who have made the effort to build apartment blocks that are designed and landscaped in accordance with at least some basic Feng Shui principles. These will have taken basic guidelines into account. I no longer find it surprising to see winding approach roads, verdant foliage, impressive main entrance ways, and softly cascading artificial waterfalls.

Many property developers now avoid designing apartment blocks that have irregular shapes which generally have some luck *missing*. Irregular shapes which also require all sorts of feng shui *cures*.

Apartment blocks, like the one shown on the right, that are built with gardens and pools especially in the centre representing a *"courtyard"* are good Feng Shui.

The presence of trees which look healthy and green always adds to the attractiveness of any condominium complex since trees are often conducive to the flow of *chi,* and are effective protection against bad *Sha Chi* which may be coming from structures, angles or roads nearby. Finally the presence of a gently curving pool introduces views of water to the residents, thereby

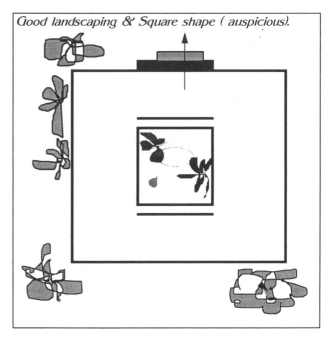

Good landscaping & Square shape (auspicious).

enhancing the Feng Shui of the surroundings. This is a good example of a complex which makes the attempt to harmonise with nature.

Next consider the proposed colour scheme of the apartment building. Does it blend with the surroundings and give one a pleasing sense of balance ? In checking out this aspect, as well as the aspect of directions, you might want to check the characteristics of any apartment building against your own personal Element and birthdate, to ensure that your personal Horoscope is compatible with the dimensional characteristics & design of the building you are contemplating living in.

How do you check this ?

Basically through your date of birth. This allows you to investigate the most auspicious and inauspicious directions. By investigating your personal auspicious directions, you will considerably enhance your practice of feng shui. However, to do this you need to refer to a Book on Compass Feng Shui. My second book entitled APPLIED PA KUA LO SHU FENG SHUI deals exclusively with this very important and vital aspect of Feng Shui practice. It also containes the full formula as well as comprehensive guidelines on how to tap your auspicious directions.

It is the only book of its kind written in English and those seriously interested in practicing Compass Feng Shui are advised to try and get a copy of this book.

Knowing your own auspicious directions enable you to very quickly check whether the main entrance of any apartment block will be lucky or unlucky for you.

Another approach is to investigate which of the 5 Elements is good for you. (See Part One, the section on The Five Elements)

EXAMPLE: If you were born in a FIRE year, then an apartment block with blue as the dominant colour is not going to be very good for you since it represents the element Water which destroys Fire; On the other hand if you were a Wood person thus such a block would be quite ideal since water is good for Wood. Similarly a building that is predominantly white represents the element Metal, and will be good for Water people, but bad for Wood people.

ASSESSING COMMON AREAS OF APARTMENT BLOCKS

The common areas of a condominium development are the service facilities that have been built into the development, the lobby or foyer area, main entrance, the lift areas, the corridors, staircases, the roof lines, and the parking areas. Many modern day condominium complexes also offer sports facilities.

Swimming pools are generally favourable, especially for those apartments that have a view of it. If the pool is a nice kidney or rounded shape so much the better. If it is rectangular, then the corners of the pools should not be facing your apartment. The size of Pools should also harmonise with the building and should not be too small or too large. If, in addition to the pool there is also landscaping which includes fountains and waterfalls then it is very good Feng Shui.

Jogging trails, especially if they are winding and gently sloping and have garden lights fitted along the way, are good Feng Shui, as these conduct healthy *chi*. Tennis courts are acceptable. Just make sure the corners do not point towards your apartment. Indoor squash and badminton courts do not have good or bad effects.

Ideally, there should be a generous entrance lobby area, since this represents the main front entrance of all the residents living in the condominium block. Generally the rules governing the main doors and entrances of houses apply in the same manner, except that for buildings the main door can be designed in a *"grander"* fashion, which will not overwhelm the building.

A <u>solid main door is always preferable to glass doors</u>, and it should not face a straight road, nor be at the junction of two or three roads. These have a negative effect on the residents because these roads are construed as "*threatening*".

There should also not be any other object or structure facing the main door which can be construed as poison arrows. In fact if the main entrance to your apartment block opens to an empty area, or a park, or a field, it is construed as very auspicious.

Upon entering the apartment block, you also should NOT directly encounter the staircase directly facing the door. This is truly most inauspicious, and the nearer the staircase is to the entrance, the more unlucky it is ! When I visited St Petersburg in Russia, one of the things I observed when I visited the old palace of the last Tsar Nicholas, was a massive grand staircase which started almost immediately from the entrance, and the offending staircase went up for three floors ! It is no wonder that the Tsar's family were constantly ill, and also that he and his family were completely wiped out !

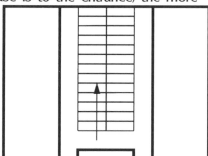

Staircase directly facing entrance is bad

The *shar chi* created for everyone living any building with this feature will be quite damaging indeed ! Examine the sketch shown above and make certain any apartment you are checking out does <u>not</u> demonstrate this feature !

Common staircases should be located by the sides of the building, and definitely should not face the Main door. Your own apartment entrance door should also not face the staircase.

Generally staircases, should not be carriers of stagnating *chi*. They should thus be well lighted and well ventilated, and ideally be closed off from the living quarters.

Lift areas and common corridors should not be too narrow, too low or too dark. Usually, these areas should suggest some life. Dark low corridors are always regarded as creating stagnating *chi*. Corridors should ideally be brightly lighted.

Apartment Entrance doors leading off from lift areas and corridors should also be aligned directly across each other. Otherwise it will not be conducive to a friendly environment.

Doors that are not aligned directly apposite each other create conflict, and if there are too many doors along a long corridor, there will be no peace and the residents will tend to quarrel with each other.

In fact it is better if there are no long corridors at all, because long corridors can also be construed to be purveyors of bad *chi*.

Condominiums with flat roofs suggest hills that have flat plateaux, and these are not very favourable. However flat roofs are preferable to roof lines which are too sharply angled. The ideal is to have a gentle sloping roof line, thus representing the gentle undulating mountain shapes that are so popular with Feng Shui practitioners.

In recent years the pyramid shaped roof has become very popular, due no doubt to the increasingly wide held belief that the ancient pyramids of Egypt represented very auspicious shapes. To the Chinese Feng Shui men, pyramid shapes are also favourable as they are usually balanced and gentle sloping.

However, it should not be forgotten that pyramids are associated with the tombs of the pharoahs, and are thus considered as *a house for the dead, a yin building !* From this perspective, I am not very keen on living or working in any buyilding which has a pyramid roof since I prefer to dwell in the *houses of the living* rather than in the *houses of the dead !*

Finally the parking areas of a condominium development should ideally be located outside the building, or under the ground level in basements, since Feng Shui guidelines generally tell us to avoid having the *"bottom"* ground levels empty; and car parks are considered to be empty areas. In Hong Kong e.g., this aspect of Feng Shui is particularly emphasised especially for office buildings or commercial blocks.

Several examples of such buildings with *"empty"* bases were pointed out to me together with the number of businesses located in such buildings which had gone bankrupt.

Therefore be wary of apartment blocks which have car park floors below the apartments themselves, unless these car park floors are built below ground. This is because car park floors are deemed to be *"empty"* so that the apartments above are sitting on insecure foundation. Even for individual houses Feng Shui masters usually advise against siting one's bedroom or important rooms above the garage.

Apartment Entrance doors leading off from lift areas and corridors should also be aligned directly across each other. Otherwise it will not be conducive to a friendly environment.

Doors that are not aligned directly apposite each other create conflict, and if there are too many doors along a long corridor, there will be no peace and the residents will tend to quarrel with each other.

In fact it is better if there are no long corridors at all, because long corridors can also be construed to be purveyors of bad *chi*.

Condominiums with flat roofs suggest hills that have flat plateaux, and these are not very favourable. However flat roofs are preferable to roof lines which are too sharply angled. The ideal is to have a gentle sloping roof line, thus representing the gentle undulating mountain shapes that are so popular with Feng Shui practitioners.

In recent years the pyramid shaped roof has become very popular, due no doubt to the increasingly wide held belief that the ancient pyramids of Egypt represented very auspicious shapes. To the Chinese Feng Shui men, pyramid shapes are also favourable as they are usually balanced and gentle sloping.

However, it should not be forgotten that pyramids are associated with the tombs of the pharoahs, and are thus considered as *a house for the dead., a yin building !* From this perspective, I am not very keen on living or working in any buyilding which has a pyramid roof since I prefer to dwell in the *houses of the living* rather than in the *houses of the dead !*

Finally the parking areas of a condominium development should ideally be located outside the building, or under the ground level in basements, since Feng Shui guidelines generally tell us to avoid having the *"bottom"* ground levels empty; and car parks are considered to be empty areas. In Hong Kong e.g., this aspect of Feng Shui is particularly emphasised especially for office buildings or commercial blocks.

Several examples of such buildings with *"empty"* bases were pointed out to me together with the number of businesses located in such buildings which had gone bankrupt.

Therefore be wary of apartment blocks which have car park floors below the apartments themselves, unless these car park floors are built below ground. This is because car park floors are deemed to be *"empty"* so that the apartments above are sitting on insecure foundation. Even for individual houses Feng Shui masters usually advise against siting one's bedroom or important rooms above the garage.

A VIEW OF WATER
ENHANCES THIS APARTMENT BUILDING

The gently curving pool located within view of the apartment units make this development an agreeable place to make one's home. Most of the residents will participate in the prosperity bringing *chi* generated by the pool.

In addition, the building itself is well balanced with regular shaped windows and nicely rounded balconies. Residents on the lower floors can also install mirrors within their individual units to *reflect* the pool into their homes, thereby further capturing the beneficial effects of the water. To ensure that the *chi* always stays healthy, it is important that the pool be properly maintained so that the water remains clean and clear at all times.

ASSESSING INTERIORS

Ensuring there is good Feng Shui harmony inside the home is just as relevant as external landscape considerations. For Apartment dwellers, considerations of Internal Feng Shui become even more important since for them applicable external factors are often difficult to assess.

The interiors of condominiums should therefore be examined carefully. The idea is to see whether the traffic flow, layout and dimensions of rooms are conducive to good Feng Shui.

The approach to adopt when examining internal Feng Shui is to strive to ensure that good, positive and healthy dragon's breath, the Cosmic *chi* can enter the home and is able to flow nicely within the home, going from room to room, without it being "*attacked*" by poison arrows, and without it stagnating.

This is achieved by following general guidelines which can be implemented without too much difficulty. Consider the following:

Good healthy *chi* always enters through the FRONT DOOR ; Thus front doors must be welcoming and open into relatively spacious and visually balanced and well lighted interiors (Sketch A). They should open inwards so that the approach of *chi* is smooth.

If on entering, (Sketch B) one encounters a wall, or a narrow corner, then the flow of *chi* is affected, and residents will suffer from ill health and have their luck "*choked*" off.

In such a situation you can consider installing a mirror although a mirror directly facing the main door is not always regarded as favourable either. The best solution really is to hang a very bright light to light up the small narrow space. If you wish to install a mirror, you can do so, but it should nto directly face the door (shown as dotted line in B) !

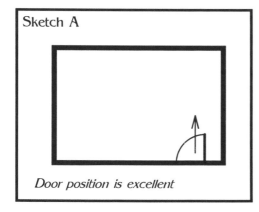

Sketch A

Door position is excellent

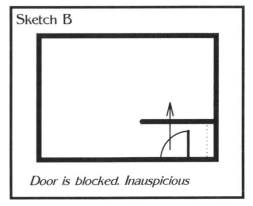

Sketch B

Door is blocked. Inauspicious

Chi also enters through the WINDOWS of one's home. But these are the secondary entrances and they should not be so large as to overwhelm the front door. Nor be so small that they suppress the inflow of Chi. The ratio of windows to doors should not exceed 3:1 as a rule of thumb.

Healthy chi can never flow in a straight line, since such a flow will be too fast and *chi* quickly dissipates. Thus room layouts must ensure that the entrance to and exits from rooms should never be in a straight line. The worst type of configuration is to have three doors opening in a row, especially if this involves both the front and back doors.

If this occurs *chi* goes in and out of the house so fast, residents will not enjoy any benefits, and indeed could even have a series of recurring problems.

If you are already living in a flat with this problem either use a screen to *"block off"* the middle doorway thus forcing *chi* to flow round it, (dotted lines) or hang a windchime or crystal from the tops of the doorways, (marked Y) thus encouraging the *chi* to pause and circulate. See sketch on the right.

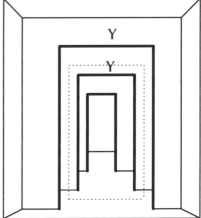

✿ *Chi* should move slowly and be encouraged to take a winding path, but its flow should not be *"blocked"* by too many obstacles in the shape of sharp corners, abrupt turns or protruding furniture.

✿ The flow of *chi* must be smooth and balanced. When the flow of *chi* is blocked the effect is usually felt in the residents' marriage and financial affairs. Tight corners can usually be *"enlarged"* with the use of mirrors, while furniture arrangement can be adjusted to ensure no blockages occur.

✿ *Chi* tends to stagnate in places or corners which are perpetually dark, or unused or still, with no life. Thus rooms should generally be well lighted and should be used; In parts of the home which are seldom used (store rooms, guest rooms), make sure they are well lighted and give these rooms an airing at least once a month. Also keep such rooms free of dust so that the smell of the rooms is not dank and dirty.

✿ *Chi* also likes sunlight (which is natural light) but not the glare of direct afternoon sun. Hence the home should not be completely shaded from the sun, nor should it be completely exposed to strong sunlight throughout the day. If the former, dampness takes place and this contributes to the creation of stagnant, tired *chi*, which will bring bad luck. At all times seek to achieve a good balance of yin with yang. Sunlight is yang, and dampnes is yin !

If there is too much sunlight (especially hot afternoon sun), there will be no balance and residents will suffer from too much Yang, causing oppressive headaches, bad tempers and continuos problems. Strong sunlight also cause furniture and furnishings to fade, and *chi* gets tired and faded as well. If you are suffering from this kind of problem, one of the best solutions is to hang a well cut lead crystal ball from the windows. This has the effect of transforming the oppressive sunlight into a rainbow of happy colours, immediately enhancing the room with revitalised and healthy *chi.*

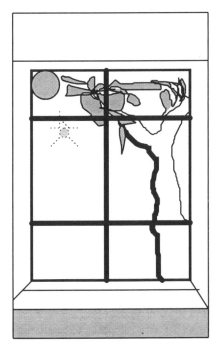

✿ Colours of walls and ceilings should be balanced such that there are healthy amounts of Yin and Yang, dark and light colours. Having a preponderance of a single colour overwhelms the home with too much Yin or too much Yang, and while this may sometimes look good, and very *"designer"* oriented, it can harmful from a Feng Shui point of view.

If the entire apartment is painted a light colour (e.g. white), this can be balanced out with the furniture, the carpets or wood flooring.

✿ Healthy c*hi* is often attracted into homes where there is life and movement and sound. Big family households have no worry on this score but in the case of young couples who work, the home is usually left quiet and silent throughout the day, and sometimes even through the evenings. Feng Shui practitioners therefore recommend leaving the radio on, hanging wind chimes that tinkle with the breeze and even advocate the keeping of fish in bubbling aquariums.

Having live plants scattered through the flat is also a good idea. These are things that suggest some form life in the home, thereby attracting good *chi.*

In Hong Kong, many residents of flats install miniature fountains which combine this aspect of Feng Shui with water which represents money. Such fountains (which are only about one foot square in size) are also believed to increase turnover for businesses.

✿ *Chi* is very vulnerable to poison arrows; thus apartment dwellers must check for sharp protruding edges that are caused by square pillars, projecting alcoves, extended corners, exposed beams, and window grills which have sharp protruding designs, even before the furniture comes in. *Sharp columns should be wrapped with mirrors.Edges can also be camouflaged with plants*

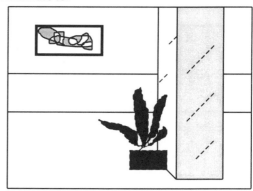

Most homes usually have at least some of these features and where they are present, you should ask yourself whether they can be effectively *"camouflaged"* or hidden by plants and creepers, and whether your furniture can be arranged such that residents will not be too badly affected by the negative vibrations caused by such edges.

Feng Shui practitioners often hang bamboo flutes on exposed beams or install specially designed tassels/curtains to soften the edges of beams and pillars.

* Apartments with one level floors are preferable to multiple or split level floors. Multiple levels cause imbalance in the home generally leading to volatility in the lives, opportunities and successes of the residents i.e. with lots of ups and downs. If there are split levels however, do make sure that the kitchen, the dining room and the bedrooms are on the higher levels.

✿ Duplex apartments or apartments with two stories require that *chi* flow upwards into the living quarters and bedrooms. In such cases the staircase within the apartment must follow some general rules. It should not rise immediately from the front door nor end upstairs directly in front of a door. Either case will bring enormous bad luck to the residents.

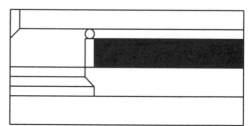

❀ Staircases should be solid (like this). They should not be too narrow, nor have spaces between the steps of the staircase as this cause the good luck *chi* to escape and never make it upstairs.

AVOID having spiral staircases, as these are generally too narrow, have spaces between the steps and resembles a corkscrew which *"twist"* at the heart of a household. Curved staircases that wind gently between two floors are the best.

In homes with split levels, make sure the dining room is located on the higher level

❀ The entire apartment should be well lighted. Try to avoid apartments with small dark corners. Check light points to ensure that this will not be a problem, since rooms and stairs which are not well lighted cause *chi* to stagnate and grow tired causing illnesses and general poor health for residents and the family.

❀ Finally make sure that the entire apartment is not too low. Modern high rises and condominiums generally build apartments which tend to have low ceilings. As long as these do not feel oppressive (i.e. relative to the height of residents, especially the head of the household) they are acceptable.

Ceiling heights which are too low, or worse, which are compounded by having wooden panelling that tend to darken the home, or have protruding corners and small rooms are oppressive, and tend to cause severe illnesses, poor health, headaches and depression.

Where this is a problem already existing in your apartment, make use of mirrors on walls to increase the feeling of space and reduce the feeling of being *"hemmed in"*.

QUICK CHECKS:
An Apartment with good Feng Shui features will a have:
* The main door opening inwards to a spacious hall.
* The doors to bedrooms properly aligned to each other.
* Well proportioned rooms.
* No protruding corners.

An apartment with Feng Shui problems will have:
* The main door opening into a narrow space. Use mirror to correct.
* Protruding corners. Use plants to camouflage.
* Three doors in a row. Use a screen or windchime.
* Too many windows. Use curtains to cover some of them.
* The toilet door too near the main door. If possible change it.
* The corridor to the bedrooms being narrow & long. Use mirrors
* Square columns which need to be camouflaged.
* The door to the kitchen opening the wrong way.
* The dining room on a lower level. Change room usage.

MAIN DOORS

should always open onto a spacious welcoming room. If it opens onto a room that is too large use a screen to create a foyer.

✿ If it opens onto a wall, use a mirror.
  ✿ If it opens into a narrow corridor, use a light or install a mirror.
  ✿ If it faces another door use windchimes or a screen.

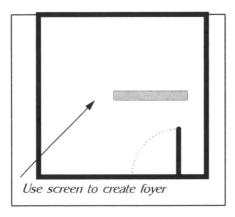

Use screen to create foyer

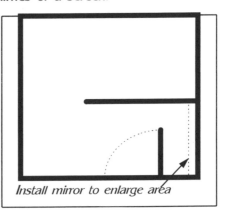

Install mirror to enlarge area

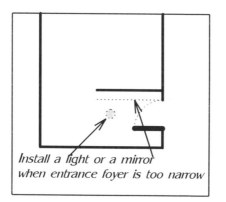

DOORs should be aligned directly opposite each other, & open into the whole room. If a door opens onto a wall, install a mirror or change the hinges.

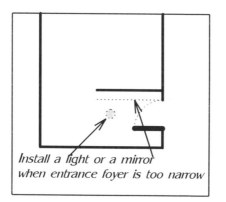

Install a light or a mirror when entrance foyer is too narrow

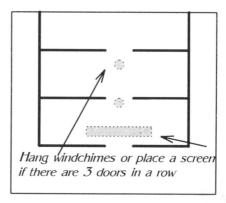

Hang windchimes or place a screen if there are 3 doors in a row

If doors are not directly aligned to each other, use mirrors.

✿ Two awkward doors blocking each other are bad.
　　Change one into a sliding door.

✿ Doors facing a window cause *chi* to flow out.
　　Put a plant by the window.

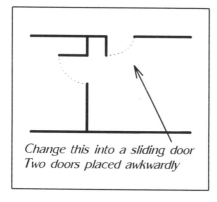

*Change this into a sliding door
Two doors placed awkwardly*

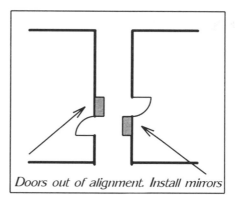

Doors out of alignment. Install mirrors

ADDITIONAL ILLUSTRATED EXAMPLES

DOORS:

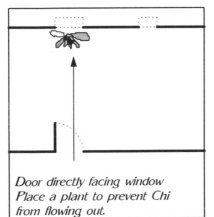

Door directly facing window
Place a plant to prevent Chi
from flowing out.

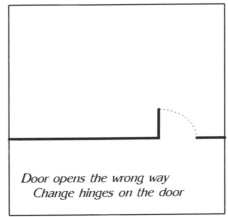

Door opens the wrong way
Change hinges on the door

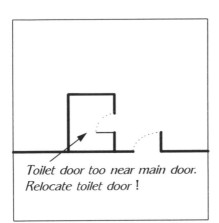

Toilet door too near main door.
Relocate toilet door !

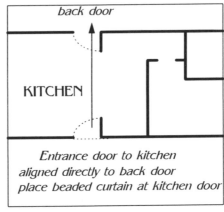

Entrance door to kitchen
aligned directly to back door
place beaded curtain at kitchen door

EXCELLENT FEATURES
IN THIS CONDOMINIUM COMPLEX

- ✿ The entrance driveway is curving and wide sloping gradually downwards bringing excellent *chi* to the entrance. All residents will benefit.
- ✿ The circular driveway with a fountain in the center allows *chi* to circulate and settle, bringing good fortune to all residents.
- ✿ The curved pool seems to embrace the building, bringing wealth to residents.
- ✿ The whole complex of buildings with multiple roof levels is well balanced. Trees, water and undulating levels reflect Nature. Distant hills also provide protection.

10. ROOM ARRANGEMENTS

The design of room layouts, particularly the placement of the important rooms, i.e. the main bedroom, the kitchen & dining room, as well as the main front door have important implications for healthy Feng Shui. This is especially true for apartment dwellers who spend all the time while at home within the confines of their home interiors having no gardens or patios. Thus the way the apartment is laid out affects the way they live and the style in which they live, both of which factors affect Feng Shui.

Thus MAIN FRONT DOORS should generally open into the more public areas of the home, i.e. the living room which is where guests and friends are entertained. If the main door opens into the dining room it is also acceptable because here is where the family (and their friends) eat, and this has pleasant connotations as well.

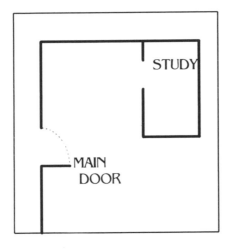

If the main door opens:
* To the STUDY, occupants will be work oriented. (Shown here)
* To the KITCHEN, occupants will tend to over eat.
* To the BEDROOM, residents will be perpetually tired.
* To the TV ROOM, occupants will fritter away their time.
* To the FAMILY ROOM, occupants will be close to each other.
* To the TOILET, residents wealth will be flushed away.

To correct any of the above situations, Feng Shui recommends the hanging of a wind Chime above the door of the room or, better yet, place a large mirror on the door itself to reflect back the main door. In designing room layouts however it is often recommended that the Main Door does not open too abruptly into another room. Far better to have the main door open into the hall or living room.

Generally the MAIN BEDROOM should be situated as far away from the Front door as possible, preferably in the diagonally opposite corner of the apartment, as shown in the diagram on the right. This gives the residents maximum control over their lives and is conducive to peace and harmony within the household. Symbolically, being away from the

Front Door also means one is more secure and can sleep more soundly at nights.

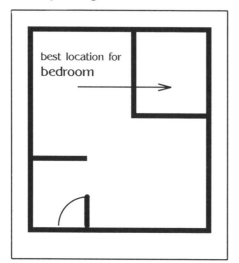
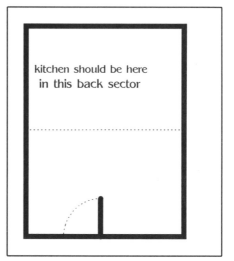

The KITCHEN should ideally be located towards the back half of the apartment, rather than be too near the entrance or in the middle of the apartment. If the kitchen is on the left of the main door as one enters the house it is also good Feng Shui as this symbolises harmony and health for the residents. Kitchens should never be narrow or confined. Spacious airy kitchens symbolise healthy *chi* for the household, and if it is too small, do not hesitate to use mirrors to "enlarge" it.

The DINING ROOM and LIVING ROOM of the home are two areas where guests are entertained. Ideally they should be next to each other. However the Dining area should always be higher than, or the same level as the Living area. Dining areas are where Feng Shui men like placing a mirror as this reflects food, thereby doubling it.

BATHROOMS and TOILETS must be located with care. As a general rule, these rooms should not be near the Entrance; nor should they be in the centre of the home. Either situation will result in the occupants wealth being flushed away. The Toilets themselves should also not be easily visible from door, and in fact hidden toilets are usually considered the best.

Some go so far as to screen off toilets with curtains.

II. FURNITURE LAYOUT

The kind of furniture and the way these are placed within the various rooms of the home have a relatively big impact on the Feng Shui of residents. Indeed sometimes, just sleeping in the wrong direction because of the way a bed has been placed can have dire consequences on careers and marriages.

Generally the approach to furniture layout is similar to that of room layout, i.e. there are some general guidelines which can be followed and adapted, after which some of the more important pieces of furniture in any household can be assessed.

All furniture placement within a home has relevance for Feng Shui. Generally however the two most important things in a residential home are the placement of the BED and the placement of the family's RICE COOKER. These two objects have the most relevance to the fortunes of a household. Notwithstanding this however, one should also be aware that depending on the condition and situation of a households existing fortunes, the Feng Shui man will also examine other furniture placements in the home to look for clues.

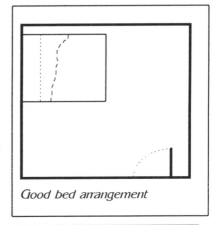

Good bed arrangement

 The BED should as far as possible be placed at the corner that is diagonally opposite the entrance to the bedroom, in any orientation, and facing any direction that is best suited to the occupant. This creates balance and allows the occupant a view of the door without at the same time being *"hit"* by *chi* entering the room. This also ensures a peaceful sleep, and by extension a peaceful life where all things proceed relatively smoothly.

If the entrance to the bedroom is not situated at a corner, or if the room

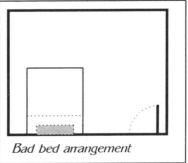

Bad bed arrangement

is not regularly shaped, then in determining the location of the bed, one should observe that it is bad Feng Shui to place the bed in a way which forces the occupant to sleep with his feet facing the door.

This is universally acknowledged as the *"death"* position, since in the old days, whenever there was a death in the family the coffin would be placed with the feet of the corpse facing the front door, i.e. getting ready to move on to the next world. Nor should the bed face the bathroom door. Subject to these two taboos, which will cause death or severe financial loss, one can then attempt to place the bed in a position which allows the occupant to have a good view of the door. Without being too close to it.

It is useful to understand that one's *"sleeping position"* has very major consequences on one's success potential, according to Feng Shui.

If the sleeping position subjects the occupant to *Sha Chi* emanating from the edges of overhanging beams or sharp corners or from poison arrows that come in through windows from a neighbouring sharp pointed structure or building, the occupant will suffer from confused thinking, illnesses, headaches and in severe cases even severe financial and career setbacks.

There will also be no harmony among family members, and husband and wife will quarrel and have strong disagreements.

The positioning of the BED should thus be made with a great deal of care. Also the view upon waking up must also be examined. Views of water, of trees, of distant mountains are auspicious. Views of buildings, especially of corners of buildings, of flyovers and straight roads are bad and such views should be blocked off with heavy drapes. It is also not advisable to place a mirror directly in front of one's BED as this leads to brutal strains in a marriage, and in extreme cases even divorce or separation of the spouses.

For students, an inauspiciously placed bed can have terrible consequences on their studies, and generally if a student who has always been doing well suddenly suffers from poor grades or has problems at school or University, it is always advisable to examine his sleeping position and the placement of his bed.

Likewise new born babies who are constantly fretful and cry incessantly through the night may be sleeping in a poorly placed bed, or is being affected by secret poison arrows emanating from protruding corners of beams.

THE OVEN OR RICE COOKER

According to Feng Shui the kitchen is one of the most important rooms in a home. As such we have seen that this must be airy, well lighted, spacious and have a regular shape. The kitchen symbolises the wealth of a family. It is where the family's food is cooked, and the quality and quantity of food available in a home strongly reflects the family's prosperity, its overall health and its well-being.

It is for this reason that Chinese families who subscribe to these beliefs always ensure that their rice urn is never empty and that the refrigerator is always well stocked.

Because food is considered so important to the Chinese, Feng Shui men always insist that the kitchen should always be brightly lit to attract a good dose of *chi*, which will then make its way into the food, thus enhancing the luck of all the occupants.

Central to all the meals in a *Chinese* household is the RICE COOKER. This is because rice is the main and staple food, and all meals are served with rice. The position of the Rice Cooker is thus exceptionally important. To start with, the Rice Cooker should always be placed in such a way that the Cook will not have his back towards the kitchen's entrance door. In a western home where the OVEN is all important, this *rule* applies to the placement of the oven.

The Rice Cooker or Oven should at all times be working nicely. If it keeps breaking down, better to purchase a new one, since a cooker or oven which constantly gets spoilt does not bode well for the family's fortunes.

These cooking machines should also at all times be clean, and the rice that is cooked daily should not be too soggy or too hard. Feng Shui men also believe that the daily bubbling of rice with water, in the Cooker if it takes place in a happy kitchen will bring continuos good luck to the family.

THE DINING TABLE

The Dining Table should stand in a room which is not too large nor too small for it. Thus, the Dining set must be well proportioned to the Dining Room. Mirrors in the Dining Room are always good Feng Shui, as it represents a doubling of the family's wealth.

Usually the Chinese do not like dining rooms to be completely enclosed as this will cause opportunities for making money to "close up ". Thus in most homes, the dining area is often just an extension of the living room.

There are four excellent shapes for Dining tables, i.e. the ROUND, the SQUARE, the RECTANGLE if its not too long, and the perfect PAK KUA. All other shapes are not recommended, especially those shapes that have their corners cut off.

Dining tables can have a single base stand or have four or six legs. Many wealthy families use large round rosewood tables, with a solid central base and stand. Often auspicious symbols are carved onto these tables, and the most popular subject is usually the dragon, especially two dragons portrayed as fighting for the pearl. It is believed that having such auspicious carvings on the Dining Room furniture further enhances one's luck.

The Dining Table can sometimes be supplemented with a sideboard or side table. As long as this does not make the room appear crammed, it is acceptable.

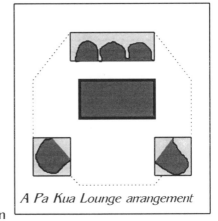

A Pa Kua Lounge arrangement

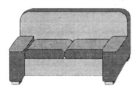

THE LOUNGE SET & COFFEE TABLE ARRANGEMENT

Furniture in the living area affects the social life of the household, especially relationships with friends and relatives. The placement of the sofas, settees and coffee tables in the living room can either enhance relationships or cause conflicts and hostilities. There are some hard and fast rules as to the general arrangement of lounge sets, and Feng Shui guidelines also tell us that certain arrangements should be avoided.

Good arrangements always ensure that none of the chairs or sofas have their backs directly facing the door or entrance way into the living room. Nor should the chairs be too close to the coffee table and the other chairs. The chairs also not be directly under beams, nor face any protruding corners.

In general arrangements that attempt to simulate the 8 sided Pak Kua shape are healthy and auspicious. Regular shaped arrangements are also good.

The L shaped type arrangement is actively discouraged unless the sofas are placed against a corner of the room. This is because this shape resembles an arrow which is not conducive to the smooth flow of *Chi.*. The sketch here shows an L shaped lounge set arrangement with the direction of poison arrows indicated to show the flow of *shar chi* created by the arrangement.

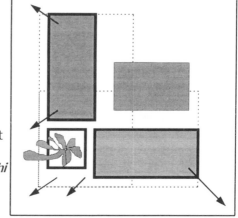

Inauspicious layout of lounge set

Legend has it that when the humble carp swims through the Celestial gates, it becomes transformed into a dragon. In ancient times, scholars who passed the Imperial exams to qualify for lofty careers were likened to the carp swimming through the heavenly gates ... In those days when emperors ruled, court advisors had to pass examinations that required deep knowledge of China's Classics, one of which was the Book of Changes or I Ching
Those who sought to attain high positions at court had to have the ability to interpret the predictions revealed through the I Ching, an important component of which entailed knowledge of feng shui.

PART FIVE

12 FENG SHUI FOR BUSINESS

In recent years, Increasingly large numbers of business people in Hong Kong, Taiwan and Singapore have actively adhered to Feng Shui principles when setting up their offices, premises, shops and factories. Many of them believe that Feng Shui can greatly enhance or seriously destroy their business luck. Thus, to avoid the collapse of business ventures, to ensure the smooth running of their enterprises and indeed, to secure prosperity and success for themselves, they go to great lengths to make certain that their place of work and business are oriented according to good Feng Shui.

In Hong Kong one of the most celebrated *believers* of Feng Shui are the Tai Pans of the Hong Kong Bank. Each succeeding Executive Chairman of this hugely successful bank has abided by the advice of the Bank's Feng Shui experts. Thus only auspicious dates are selected for important moves made, while the two Guardian Lions which protect the bank's fortunes are placed according to Feng Shui orientations.

Its head office building in the Central District of Hong Kong Island enjoys an unencumbered view of the Harbour to protect its wealth. This, the Bank has assured by donating the land to the Government with the provision that no one may build on it. Plans for its new corporate headoffice Building in the Central District, were also vetted by Feng Shui men before construction began as well as throughout the construction period.

They are thus the most prominently known customer of Feng Shui expertise in Hong Kong. Their senior executives make sure that every major business *move* gets the Feng Shui green light.

I once asked Willie Purves the Bank's present Chairman if he personally believed in Feng Shui and his answer, *'I don't disbelieve it... but here at the Hong Kong Bank it is almost a tradition.* Indeed its many Chinese customers and staff would not have it any other way.
Old timers at the Bank recall how, many years ago the Hong Kong Bank managed to *swallow* up the colony's second largest bank, the Hang Seng Bank (which is now a subsidiary) because the latter had a terrible run. Caused, the story goes by the poor Feng Shui of the then Hang Seng Bank's head office building.

Its entrance way, the story goes, had been flanked by two huge pillars which resembled two deadly wedges *forcing open* its mouth (because the design of escalators near the entrance made them look like teeth. Thus the mouth seemed to stay open, unable to close, thus causing the money to run out !!. Hang Seng Bank is considered one of the Colony's best managed banks, but its bank run of those days is one of many feng shui stories of that colony.

In Taipei, evidence of the practice of Feng Shui is freely available in the commercial areas of the city. Here the visitor will notice that the corners of Buildings are usually *rounded* out so that *poison arrows* are not created nor pointed at neighbours. This ensures that the Pak Kua mirror is not used in retaliation, always a possibility in this very feng shui conscious business environment ! There is also the wide use of large revolving doors in front of office blocks and corporate headquarters. It is believed that revolving doors help create good *chi* for the buildings concerned. The revolving movement is also believed to be good for *chi* to travel into the building as it slows it down, therby making it friendly and auspicious.

In many of the leading hotels in both Singapore and Hong Kong, visitors will observe that almost all the huge columns or massive pillars in lobbies are either wrapped around with mirrors or have their edges *rounded* off, again reflecting attempts to do away with *poison arrows* caused by the sharp edges of these pillars. Or huge plants are used to block off angles and dissipate the bad luck effect of pointed corners.

In Malaysia, Feng Shui has also been widely practised by *Chinese* business people, and there are several *stories* about Feng Shui having gone wrong for some of the Tycoons who have lost their fortunes. The tabloid press here have often speculated about the excellent Feng Shui created for Genting Highlands by its brilliant founder Tan Sri Lim Goh Tong, in that the shape of the first hotel built up at Genting was *all embracing*, its two *wings* formed in a welcoming gesture.

They speculate also about the fervent belief in Feng Shui shown by his very successful daughters, Datin T H Tan of Southern Bank, and SK Lim of Metroplex, both of whom it is said would not make any changes to their residences or offices without consulting the Feng Shui man.

There is also the true story of the Hong Leong Dragon. In the mid Eighties at a time when Malaysia was going through severe Recession which also affected the Hong Leong Group here, a Feng Shui expert from Hong Kong informed senior officers of the Group that its logo, the Dragon had been drawn to look like a hungry, poor dragon.

It was also enclosed inside a circle thus making it impossible for it to fly and grow. The Logo was then redrawn to transform the dragon into a prosperous looking, smiling creature and the dreaded circle removed. The Hong Leong Group has not looked back since and has grown from strength to strength.
Take a look at the Hong Leong dragon logo today. It is reproduced here on the left !

The Hong Leong Dragon

Then there is of course the story of the spectacular collapse of the Carrian Group in Hong Kong. According to local gossip, George Tan, the head of Carrian had managed to get away with his countless "shady" deals because he had enjoyed excellent Feng Shui.

Until a road flyover was constructed in front of his Building. This flyover resembled the *pincers of a giant crab*, with the Carrian Building caught helplessly in its grasp. As a result, shortly thereafter, the Group collapsed with all its shocking aftermath and repercussions !
Truth or Feng Shui folk lore ?

How Feng Shui actually works has never been satisfactorily explained. Business people who believe in it however do not attempt to explain the hows and the whys. They believe in Feng Shui purely out of faith in an ancient practise which they are confident actually creates good vibes or bad vibes depending on whether they get their Feng Shui right or wrong.

The famed Singapore writer, Evelyn Lip who has made a lifetime's study of Feng Shui as it relates to Business in order to incorporate it into her professional work as an architect believes that Feng Shui leads to good aesthetic sense in architecture. She maintains that good Feng Shui brings about a sense of equilibrium, which in turn leads to clear mindedness and ultimately to success.

This is of course attributed to the basic principles of Feng Shui, that of harmony and balance, good proportions and regular shapes, equal emphasis being given to nature and the environment, and ultimately the striving to achieve a unified wholeness and integration of parts to create a harmonious existence within the Universe.

Add to this the other aspects of Chinese philosophy which borrows so much from superstitious folk lore and ancient tradition, and we have today an "accepted body of practices" which represent good Feng Shui.

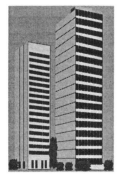

COMMERCIAL BUILDINGS

Good Feng Shui for Commercial Buildings follows the same principles which have been covered in earlier chapters for houses, apartment blocks and link houses. In locating commercial centres, once again it is important to find the *green dragon* and the *white tiger*, and thereafter to locate the areas of maximum *chi* creation.

As a rule of thumb, the land to the left of the building can represent the dragon and therefore should be slightly higher than the land on the right, which can represent the white tiger. Some Feng Shui experts even go so far as to suggest that this *dragon/tiger* symbolism can be represented by the heights and colours of the buildings to the left and right of ones location.

If in city centres, look around at the neighbouring buildings. Identify the tallest and most prominent buildings nearby, and see if they are built in harmony with nature. Is there life in the buildings nearby ?

∗ Are there open and semi open spaces
  that have been landscaped to create Yin and Yang balance ?
∗ Are the roads and covered walkways,
  pedestrian paths and steps linked in a harmonious way ?
∗ Is there enough light and plant life to create *breathing areas* ?

If the neighbouring buildings and area are nicely balanced, the next thing to do is to observe whether there are hills and waterways nearby. If so check whether your building can be oriented in a way which lets it face the water and have its back to the hills. By doing this you will be enhancing the Feng Shui potential of your building.

On the other hand a building should never face a hill as this blocks off all the good luck. At the same time if its back is to the waterway, then residents in the building will see opportunities but be unable to grasp them. This is because water flowing past the sides or backs of buildings do not bring success enhancing *chi*. The water must flow past the front door of the building.

Potentially however, most auspicious to any site is the presence of slow flowing meandering rivers which can be utilised to greatly improve the building by incorporating the view of the river in the building plan. If your building site is near a river therefore, it is eminently worthwhile to bring in a Feng Shui expert who can calculate the best means to harness the good effects of the water.

> ❀ *I have written an entire book devoted to the formulas of Water Feng Shui and its applications to trap and harness immense wealth luck. Good water feng shui has to do with direction of its flow pass the main entrance of buildings, its exit directions and its balance with the surrounding environment. Water Feng Shui is, however a very advanced branch of the science, as its effective implementation does require at least a basic understanding of basic feng shui principles !*

MERGING WITH THE EXISTING BUILDINGS.

Feng Shui has to do with the shapes and forms of the built up environment, and no single building can be assessed on its own as a solitary entity. Hence in designing your own commercial structure, or in assessing any building within which to place your office, shop or showroom, it is important to examine how the building being assessed fits in with the other buildings around you. Look at the picture above. It shows very tall & massive buildings next to very low buildings. This actually causes imbalance and is not very auspicious to the low building, whose *chi* flows will be overwhelmed by the taller and more massive buildings next door.

Consider some of these guidelines:

✪ Firstly it is undesirable to construct a series of commercial buildings in varying heights, shapes, sizes and forms which are visually unrelated and worse, which are in disharmony, i.e. with angles pointed at each other and building lines forming corners that *hit* at each other. This sort of imbalance, which is quite common in certain parts of any City is bad Feng Shui. Fortunately the ill effects of this kind of landscape can be nullified by the generous planting of trees which in effect cause the imbalance to dissipate as the branches and leaves of the trees sway in the breeze. This has happened in parts of Kuala Lumpur City, and also in prosperous Singapore.

✪ Secondly it is undesirable to construct buildings which have differing heights as this suggests imbalance in that it seems as if *something is missing*. Some sceptics have indicated that such a design suggests steps upwards and hence should augur well for the residents, but Feng Shui experts say that steps do not just go up, they go down as well, and many experts believe that in the long run, buildings that have this step feature do not represent good feng shui since it is fundamentally not demonstrative of balance. Look at the buildings shown below.

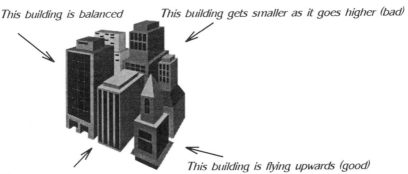

This building is balanced   *This building gets smaller as it goes higher (bad)*

This building is flying upwards (good)

This building is hemmed in (not so good)

✪ Thirdly, buildings that are constructed close to each other, and especially, rows of shophouses, should ideally have similar proportions i.e. they should be of the same width in their frontage, the same heights in the number of levels they have and also the same length.

SHOPHOUSES

Good harmonious proportions is always good Feng Shui and augurs well for the businesses in all the shops. Thus if you own a shop within a row of shophouses, you are strongly advised not to divide your shop front into two, as if undertaking two types of business. If you do this then your frontage has in effect become narrower than those of your neighbouring shops and this works against you.

Similarly if your neighbouring shops use two shoplots to create a larger frontage, this too will be bad for you AND good for your neighbour since your shoplot will then be narrow when compared to that of your neighbour.

In assessing shophouses with a view to renting them for commercial businesses, always examine the neighbouring shops as well, not only to make sure that your businesses will be compatible but also that you will not in any way have problems arising from your neighbour's business or his Feng Shui.

✪ Fourthly, commercial buildings should never be the cause of bad sha *chi* or *poison arrows* to neighbouring buildings. This often causes the neighbours to *retaliate* often without you even knowing, since it is done with the powerful Pa Kua mirror which reflects all the bad *chi* back to you. Sometimes the retaliation is so hostile (e.g when a cannon is used) your business will take a turn for the worse, you will find it difficult to recover. Its like being seriously injured !

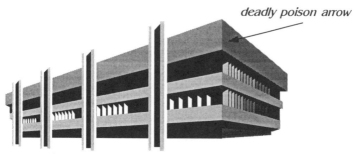

deadly poison arrow

Can you spot the poison arrows emanating from this building ? If something like this is near your building make sure you are not being hit directly by the sharp, fierce looking arrow pointed outwards !

Sharp corners and pointed rooflines often cause this. So also does reflective, mirrored glass which creates blinding glare to neighbours. If the reflective glass does not cause glare, it is not a source of sha *chi*, and is acceptable.

✪ Fifthly NEVER locate your building, or your office in a building, which directly faces a T junction, particularly one where the traffic is coming towards you. This same principle is also true of shops within shopping complexes. This is because the *chi* created at such junctions is too strong, too vibrant, and is often poisonous, thus causing very bad luck. This building here is being hit by the oncoming road !

Poison arrow at T junction

THE FROG
A FENG SHUI STORY

Mr Wu, a wealthy rice trader lived with his parents in Aberdeen. At the age of 35 he was a prosperous millionaire, drove a Mercedes Benz, had married a reasonably good looking woman who had given him three children, two of whom were boys. All he needed now was his own mansion. His wife was overjoyed when he announced his intentions, and confided that he had found a "perfect" piece of land near Discovery Bay. {PRIVATE }
As is the practice in Hong Kong he consulted a Feng Shui expert who pronounced the site "excellent", with the prerequisite green dragon white tiger formations. He also had views of the bay and from his home he could walk onto the beach or swim in the sea. The rooms were carefully situated to benefit every member of his family and in the house, he displayed all the symbols of prosperity. Mr Wu was a very happy man.

Trouble started six months later. Every member of his family became ill. His business floundered, and he himself suffered a near fatal accident. When his youngest son contracted pneumonia and died, he was convinced something was terribly wrong with the Feng Shui of his new mansion.

Mr Wu invited three Feng Shui men in succession to check out the house. Each in turn came, studied the land, the home, the surroundings and pronounced everything perfect ! Relieved, Mr Wu relaxed. Three months later his wife fell down the stairs, hit her head against the balustrade and landed in hospital in a coma. Once again Mr Wu suspected something had to be wrong with his Feng Shui. His business troubles had also got worse.

Quite by accident, Mr Wu bumped into an old friend to whom he confided his woes. The friend recommended his Feng Shui master from Taiwan who happened to be in town. "Let me bring him over this evening ", his friend said. By the time the Feng Shui man, Master Li arrived, it was dark and Mr Wu suggested he stay overnight so he could check out the house the next day.
Early the next morning Master Li woke up at six, and walking down to the beach so he could get a better view of the mansion, he was appalled to see that the tide was down, and in the sea lay a huge boulder, shaped like a frog with its mouth wide open aimed directly at the mansion, as if it was feeding from it.
Hurrying back to the house he collided with Mr Wu. "I think I have found the source of all your problems" he said with a gentle smile. Pointing to the huge rock in the sea, he said, "Get rid of that. Do it quickly, otherwise you could lose your whole family".
It did not take long to remove the rock. Mr Wu at last understood why the other Feng Shui men had missed the malevolent frog lying in the sea, hidden by the high tides. After solving the mystery, Mr Wu's wife and business quickly recovered.

In downtown Kuala Lumpur, there is a magnificent building, the <u>Arab Malaysian Bank Head Office</u> in Jalan Raja Chulan, which at first glance seems to be facing a T Junction. On closer examination however you will find that this is not so, and indeed the whole building has been oriented such that the entrance *does not face the junction*. Also the use of reflective glass in this building far from reflecting glare, instead reflects the beautiful blue sky thereby bringing auspicious Feng Shui to its residents as it is as if they are working in the sky, with lots of room to grow and expand.

Many years ago when I was a student in the United States, I visited New York a great deal, and one of the buildings I noticed then was the imposing <u>PanAM building</u> which of course was hit by the straight avenue on which it was located. I am not surprised that this once great airline suffered from so many business problems !

And of course there is also another famous example of a building which faces a straight road in London. This is none other than the regal <u>Buckingham Palace</u> which stands at the end of the Mall. If you visit the Palace do notice the straight road in front of it. This is the Mall, and it is not surprising that the British Royal family has suffered so much anguish and heartbreak through the years. Indeed if it were not for the circular roundabout right in front of the palace, which serves to mitigate some of the killing *chi* coming from the road, the problems of the Royal family would have been far worse !

FENG SHUI OF BUCKINGHAM PALACE

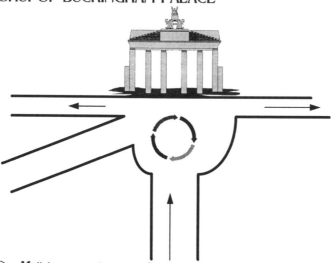

The Mall here creates a terrible poison arrow aimed directly at the Palace, although its killing breath is somewhat deflected by the roundabout in front of the palace !

From the guidelines above, it is obvious that what makes for good Feng Shui for office buildings is harmony; harmony of shapes, forms and dimensions. And also, a real absence of hostile *poison arrows* ! This is the most chilling of all feng shui taboos. If you do nothing else save protect against *poison arrows*, you would have done much to ensure that there is a good dose of good healthy *chi* flowing into your building !

Thus when assessing shopping malls and complexes, look at the overall harmony of design. Lot 10 shopping complex in Kuala Lumpur has excellent Feng Shui because the design of the entire complex does not create bad vibes for neighbours. It is a nicely curving building

Entrances into the complex are large and wide and even its driveways upto the car parks are wide and open thus allowing good *chi* to flow gently into the building. Inside the complex itself, the shoplots have been divided with a good eye for Feng Shui harmony. No single shop looks or appears unusually narrow or cramped. *Chi* flows gently from floor to floor and the escalators leading to the higher floors do not directly face the doorways of the complex.

ORIENTATIONS OF BUILDINGS
We can summarise the guidelines on building orientations as follows:

* Ideally, land and buildings on the left of the front door should be higher than land or buildings on the right,

* The front entrance of a building should not directly face a T junction.

* The front entrance of a building should not face a hill or elevated land, or a massive, disproportionately high structure.

* If possible, where there are waterways or rivers nearby the front door should be oriented to face such waterways.

* Ideally the back of the building should be supported by a hill or higher building.

* Avoid buildings which face a flyover which curves into it, or appears to *cut* into the building.

To achieve success and prosperity for its owners, buildings should, if possible, be oriented according to the horoscope of the principal owner or the most senior person in charge.

But this should be done only after taking the above guidelines into consideration. The building's front entrance should thus, ideally be designed to coincide with the direction(s) that best benefit the owner of the building ! As should of course also his private suite of offices within the building. For people renting buildings, or office suites in buildings, select one whose main entrance corresponds to your best direction, or at least try to avoid those with directions that clash with yours !

✪ *To investigate your personal auspicious and inauspicious directions according to your date of birth, please consult my second book APPLIED PA KUA LO SHU FENG SHUI which is devoted exclusively to this Compass Formula Feng Shui.*

Some Feng Shui experts orient buildings in accordance with the year of construction of the building. Those who use this method consult what is referred to as *flying star feng shui* which is also part of Compass Formula Feng Shui.

Flying Star feng shui is based on the effect of intangible forces caused by the way numbers *fly* around the building's natal chart. And the natal chart is drawn up based on when the building was built ! This branch of feng shui is widely practised in Hong Kong where feng shui masters enjoy a brisk trade calculating out the fortunes of buildings at the start of every lunar new year !

❀ *This emphasis on the time dimension of feng shui is contained in my fourth book entitled CHINESE NUMEROLOGY IN FENG SHUI. Once again this is a very advanced school of Feng Shui practice and beginners are advised to familiarise themselves with the basic and underlying concepts of feng shui before attempting to draw up natal charts for their homes and offices.*

Others follow accepted Feng Shui guidelines on directions which identify the South as the best direction and the Northwest and Southwest as the *inauspicious* directions. Generally the *Chi*nese believe that lucky and unlucky directions change from year to year, and for those who wish to put a fine point on directions, they are advised to consult either the annual *Tong Shu* which offers auspicious directions for each year, or the *I Ching* which often gives a suitable direction when *consulted.*

The Tong Shu is the Chinese Almanac which is updated annually. It contains all the information necessary to undertake all sorts of divinitive analysis that are based on Chinese cultural concepts of elements and calendar dates.The I Ching is the Book of Oracles, and it's 64 hexagrams offer every kind of advice including feng shui advice !

 POISON ARROWS

are such an integral part of feng shui that it is vital for anyone wanting to investigate their feng shui study them carefully, especially on how to recognise them ! As with houses and apartment blocks, it is necessary to examine the surrounding landscape of a building very carefully in order to identify poison arrows.

Sometimes the arrows are hidden, or are not immediately obvious. But the killing or sha *chi* which they bring your way can be quite terrible. They are also secret and intangible, and you have to be on the lookout for them. Poison arrows bring bad luck which cause businesses to collapse either by creating cash flow problems or causing everything that can go wrong to do so. What does one have to look out for ? What are the structures and objects which can hurt a building ?

Unlike a house, which in dimension is much smaller, commercial buildings, factories and other larger man made constructions, things like flag posts, lamp posts, trees etc. which would normally seriously hurt the Feng Shui of a house, would not be as powerful in their negative effects UNLESS these objects are directly facing the front door, or the front entrance of the building. And even then their effect will lack the same potency.

What DOES hurt buildings generally are the steep and pointed roof forms and roof lines, especially where the roofs come together to form a pointed triangle, and the larger, and sharper these lines are the more deadly they can be in creating bad luck. Similarly the corners of neighbouring buildings are also extremely harmful, especially when the building is very massive, and one of its corner is directly *hitting* at the front or name of the Building.

In Malaysia, along the Federal Highway to Port Klang, somewhere near the vicinity of the Shah Alam industrial estate, there is a massive building in Shah Alam town itself, which has been oriented in such a way that its sharp side sends a very powerful poison arrow directly across the road and hitting the top of the UMW factory complex located in the industrial estate in Shah Alam. In the mid Eighties the effect of this arrow was particularly potent and it hurt UMW enormously.

Today, those interested can take a drive and see this *arrow* for themselves. It is still visible from the Federal Highway. However the effects of this poison arrow has been nullified altogether with the planting of trees, whose rich foliage effectively and completely blocks off the sha *chi* making its way towards UMW.

Sometimes there may be other objects lurking nearby which can create bad *chi* to unsuspecting residents. For example one of the objects which Malaysians should beware of are antique cannons which are placed outside some buildings for aesthetic reasons. These bring terrible bad luck. An example of this is the cannon pointing at the Apera Building in Jalan Raja Chulan. The cannon does not affect the entire building but residents *within firing range* i.e. upto the fifth floor could well experience bad luck as a result of the cannon.

Other objects like steel sculptures or so called *modern art* sculptures can also sometimes represent malign forces. Indeed, I often wonder why some large corporate buildings display large sculptures that have so many pointed edges directed at their own entrance ! Naturally these are passed off as art pieces but it really is advisable to take a second look ! I have also seen other so called art pieces that resemble gravestones, arranged just in front of a building and once again I wonder why such an inauspicious arrangement has been placed there !

So be alert when you are assessing buildings. Anything sharp, or represents a knife, or can be a cutting edge are all bad !

SHAPES & FORMS

Basically, Feng Shui almost always prefers regular to irregular shapes, and symmetrical forms are always considered more auspicious than non symmetrical forms. Thus, squares, rectangles, circular shapes and also the eight sided Pa Kua shapes are all considered good and acceptable. Buildings based on these shapes generally will not have Feng Shui problems related to shapes.

This does not however mean there is no room for creativity in building design which can also be good Feng Shui. Nor does it suggest that all other shapes are automatically *bad* Feng Shui. What Feng Shui does insist on is HARMONY, i.e. the kind of harmony that is achieved by having a proper balance of dimensions, or spatial utilisation, of colours, of light, of temperature, of soft Yin lines and Yang hard lines.

Visually the *whole* must appear balanced, so that space and form and proportions are carefully integrated to create a pleasing and balanced impression. Thus the rule of thumb of symmetry is a useful starting point to judge the harmonious appearance of structures. Sometimes different geometric forms can create harmony e.g. a circular building, built in the right proportions can harmonise quite effectively with a square or rectangular structure.

HARMONIOUS INTEGRATION OF SHAPES

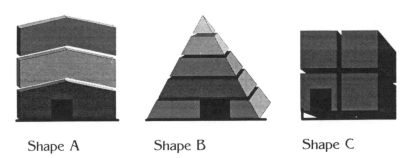

Shape A   Shape B   Shape C

Shown here are three popular integrated shapes which are regarded as fairly auspicious shapes. Shape A comprise two wings which seem to welcome the luck coming its way. If the entrance is placed in the centre here the configuration also resembles the green dragon/white tiger configuration which is considered so auspicious. Genting Hotel has this auspicious shape.

Shape B is the ever popular pyramid shape ! In feng shui terms, the pyramid is seen as a triangle shape pointing upwards which indicate growth, and is therefore good. Entrance into such a shaped building can be on either one of the four sides.

However because the pyramid also symbolises a tomb (they are after all the tombs of the ancient Egyptian kings) it is regarded as a *yin* type structure, and should thus be balanced out with yang characteristics, like having it brightly lit. The <u>pyramid in the Louvre</u> in Paris is a perfect example of a balanced pyramid made auspicious by its glass characteristic which brings all the sunlight into the building ! It has thus enjoyed extremely good business since opening !

Shape C is a very regular and symmetrical shape, made up of rectangualr blocks. This modular integration of similiar shapes is very safe and is also easy to activate from a feng shui viewpoint. If you have such a building you should make sure that you have a well defined main entrance.

It is also useful to check out the symbolism of the total configuration. Symbolism here refers to the Chinese concept of what is good or bad, what is lucky or unlucky, what is auspicious or inauspicious. Thus buildings which resemble auspicious Chinese characters that have good meanings is said to be *good*, and those which resemble Chinese characters that have bad meanings is *bad*!

GOOD & BAD SHAPES
BASED ON CHINESE CHARACTERS

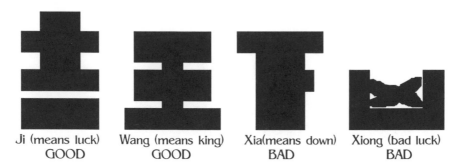

Ji (means luck)   Wang (means king)   Xia(means down)   Xiong (bad luck)
      GOOD   GOOD   BAD   BAD

Thus buildings whose structure resemble the word *"xia"* meaning going down, or the word *"xiong"* meaning bad luck are of course bad. Still on this line of thought buildings which are "decorated" with upward pointing arrows are good while downward pointing arrows are bad.

At the same time any shape which can be interpreted as being incomplete is *bad.* Like a semi circle, or a step like appearance to the building's height. Or buildings in the shape of a "T", or an "L" because here it seems as if *something is missing.*

Then again, certain shapes are supposed to be anathema to the Chinese. Like crosses and triangles. Thus buildings having these shapes are predicted to bring problems to people doing business in them. Of course the most famous building in the world which has these characteristics is the <u>Bank of China Building</u> in Hong Kong. Feng Shui Masters have given this building a mixed reaction, but the concensus is that the surrounding roads of the building are so asupicious that the building has good feng shui ! What many of them are agreed on is that the building definitely has bad feng shui for some of its neighbours, notably the <u>Governor's house</u> ! It is also interesting that its nearest neighbour, the <u>Hong Kong Hilton</u> is being torn down, ostensibly to make way for an new office building ! We shall ahve to see the eventual fate of the new building !

Finally there is the symbolism suggested by resemblance to animals or other living creatures. If your building resembles a *dragon* for example it is supposed to be good. While if it resembles a *butterfly* it is bad because a butterfly is short-lived.

THE IMPORTANCE OF LANDSCAPING

This is the most effective modern method of ensuring that commercial buildings in cities and towns can create Yin/Yang balance that leads to good *chi* flows. As a general rule, concrete structures are Yang, while plants and flowers and shrubs are Yin. Thus the introduction of vegetation goes a long way towards balancing the Yang nature of cityscapes. Usually, landscaped courtyards within buildings, or within a commercial complexes generate a great deal of healthy *chi* which is good for business.

There are several *things* that one can build into the landscaping of buildings to augment good Feng Shui. These are:

❀ Small streams and waterways that meander slowly within the
   labyrinth of plants and trees.
   Streams bring wealth to the businesses nearby.

❀ Fountains, especially rounded fountains
   which create massive amounts of good luck *chi,*
   and encourages high turnovers for businesses.

❀ Ponds for keeping good luck carp and tortoises,
   and for growing lotus blooms, all of which
   represent success, prosperity and a smooth flow for the business.

❀ Rockies and boulders to represent hills and mountains
   that also provide protection against bad luck and ill fortune.

❀ Plants and flowers to symbolise active growth & expansion.
❀ Trees to symbolise strength and integrity.
❀ Flowers to symbolise happiness and goodwill for the residents.

These *things* can be used altogether and skilfully blended in an overall design. Or they can be utilised in any combinations deemed pleasing to the eye. There are however certain *taboos* to be followed in putting these elements if landscaping together.

❋ Firstly there must be a sense of balance, not just in shapes but also in dimensions. Hence it is no use planting a particularly large tree which dwarfs everything else. There will then be no harmony.

❋ Secondly, any pond created should ideally be circular in shape and appear to be embracing the building. It should again not be too large as to dominate the entire landscape nor too small to be effective. Make sure the pond is clean and if rearing fish make sure the fish are healthy and well fed. Ponds that are allowed to get dirty with murky water create sha *chi*, i.e. poisonous breath.

❋ Thirdly, streams should meander, and should never be built in a straight line. If there are walkways built into the landscape, these too should meander, and not be straight.

To many *Chinese* the addition of decorative animals which symbolise prosperity, success, wealth or money is also good Feng Shui. Hence red bats made of porcelain or wood are often added for good luck, as are tortoises, phoenixes and dragons. Bronze representations of deer, horses, lions and unicorns symbolise luck and strength and protection.

SIGNBOARDS, LOGOS & NUMBERS.

Before going on to the interiors of offices, shops and business premises, one major aspect of Feng Shui for business is the attention being given to the company's Signboard and Logo, i.e. its design, its size, and the orientation of its placement.

The Chinese are also very particular about the name of businesses and there are many superstitious associations that are attributed to the number of strokes that make up a name as well as the symbolic representations. These do not however form part of Feng Shui practice.

Signboards and Logos however are considered vital elements of the overall Feng Shui of a business and as such due consideration has to be given to the placement and design of these. The dimensions of signboards should follow the general Feng Shui precepts of balance and harmony. Plus, if made out in specific feng shui dimensions, it will be doubly auspicious. Clarity of words and characters as well as dimensions of lettering should always reflect balance.

In selecting colours for signboards, Feng Shui experts recommend an analysis of the proprietor's Element. Thus, depending on whether one was born in the year of Wood, Fire, Water, Metal or Earth, one should choose a colour that represents the element that is compatible with one's element.

Thus if you were born in a year whose element is Wood, then you will be good for fire i.e. the colour red. Thus your signboard should be predominantly red. Or if you were born in the year which is represented by water, then you are good for wood i.e. the colour green on your signboard will mean that you will contribute to the success of your business. And so on.

Remember that the signboard represents the business, and YOU, as the managing person, i.e. as the one who runs the business must be *good* for it, not the other way around.

Some practitioners feel there are certain colours which are intrinsically *suitable* for certain types of businesses, like the colours gold and red for restaurants because fire is used to cook food; white for jewellery shops, because white represents metal and gold is metal; and so on.

The Chinese are also great believers in the use of lights. Brightly coloured lights, especially for restaurants draw in customers, and one has only to recall the gaudy bright lights of Tokyo's Ginza area to understand the magic of neon lights.

In the United States an entire gambling town, Las Vegas, was built in the desert. For those who have visited this city who can forget the bright lights there, lights that suggest activity throughout the nights and days !! Closer to home, you will find that the restaurants in Kuala Lumpur and other major towns in Malaysia which are brightly lighted do a humming business night after night.

The selection of designs to incorporate into a company's Logo is a little more complicated. While there are no hard and fast rules, remember that certain shapes are more auspicious than others. Also, that anything that seems unbalanced, incomplete or represents disharmony, or resembles an inauspicious symbol is to be avoided. Thus crosses and triangles are generally not recommended. The same is true also of downward pointing arrows.

CIRCULAR SHAPES EXCELLENT FOR LOGOS

If shapes have to be used and incorporated into logo designs, squares and circles are generally considered good shapes.

The use of good luck words in the Chinese character is also popular as it is believed to have good fortune connotations. Hence words like *double happiness* or growth or *luck* are good words to work with.

THE DRAGON & OTHER ANIMALS

Many Chinese businesses use the dragon as their logo as the dragon is generally considered an auspicious creature which symbolises power, authority, vitality and courage. Indeed the dragon is the most widely used symbol for the Chinese and in Chinatowns throughout the world this creature rears its proud head in a multitude of forms and representations, both on the outside signboards and in the interiors as part of the decor and interior design of businesses.

The logo shown here was my own Dragon Seed logo. When I took over the chairmanship of this department store chain in Hong Kong in 1987, the first thing I did was to change its logo. I wanted something which would re-vitalise this sleepy company which had such excellent name acceptance amongst the rich housewives of the colony, but which, when we bought in was demonstrating lethargy ! I needed desperately to jazz up its image ! The choice of the dragon was obvious - but what sort of dragon ? Because we sold very upmarket goods, I decided I wanted something which suggested class and prestige, and what better way than to suggest a crown ?

But I also wanted the dragon. And I wanted something auspicious ! So we hit on a frolicking, happy dragon ! And we used silver and purple as our colours ! The direct literal translation of these colours in Cantonese meant money or ngan chee ! (ngan is silver and chee is purle !) and this colour combination has also been used for this book !

THE DRAGON SEED LOGO

The phoenix, tortoise, lion, bat and deer are also considered good luck symbols, and they make excellent logos, as they represent continuity and strength, determination and material wealth.

GEOMETRIC & ABSTRACT DESIGNS

When it comes to geometric and abstract designs do be careful not to get too carried away. Sometimes, without realising it, one can adopt a logo which can be extremely inauspicious like the logo of Supreme corporation which resembled a *broken Pa Kua*, a very inauspicious symbol. This is because the Pa Kua has always represented an object of defence, widely used by Feng Shui believers to counteract poison arrows and other symbols of danger that create sha or bad *chi*. For it to be broken suggests that it has *lost* to the forces of bad *chi*.

NUMBERS
Finally a brief discussion of numbers.

To the Chinese, especially those in Hong Kong, certain
9999   numbers are more auspicious than others, and at the
top of the list of excellent numbers is nine. Nine represents the fullness
of heaven and earth; it is the largest number and whether it be one,
two, three or four nines, they still add up to nine, thus imbuing the
number with magical connotations. Thus 9 plus nine equals 18, and
then again 1 plus 8 equals. Try the same thing with 9 plus 9 plus 9; it
equals 27, and these two numbers added together make up 9 again.
And so forth.

In Hong Kong one of the most high profile successful entrepreneurs
there is Dickson Poon. His personal Rolls Royce has the number
9999, for which he told me he paid a million dollars for. In the years I
have followed his progress I have seen him go from strength to
strength, each year overcoming one crisis after another because
something always happens to save him, and pull him out of a credit
crunch. When I knew him all he owned were fifteen rented boutiques.
Today he sits as Executive Chairman of Dickson Concepts Limited, a
multi billion dollar company which owns 100 % of ST Du Pont of Paris
with its world wide network of boutiques, and the upmarket London
department store, Harvey Nichols.

I have never forgotten what he told me about his 9999 car, that it
brings him great good luck and immense wealth. His other cars, and
he has an entire fleet of Lamborginis, Porches, Corniches and
Mercedes Benzes all carry the number 928, an excellent combination
of numbers which literary means *"Bounteous easy growth &*
expansion", the meaning gleaned from a play of the sounds of the
numbers in the Cantonese dialect.

Coming a close second to nine, is of course the number 8. Indeed
there are those who believe 8 is even more superior than 9. When
combined with other numbers, 48 is good because it means a lot of
growth, and 28 is good because it means easy growth, but 58 is not
good because it means no growth. The number 3 is also considered
auspicious for it connotes new beginnings, but it is not as highly
desired as the number 8.

To the *Chinese*, the number 4 is avoided at all costs because it literally
means *death*. Thus 24, which means easy death, or 174, which means
all dying together are to be avoided at all costs.

Numbers take on significance when they are put on your cars; are the end digits of your telephone or fax numbers; is part of your address; or are the end digits of your credit cards or bank accounts.

Business people who follow Feng Shui considerations are usually fussy about these numbers in their business life. It is for these reasons that most banks today who are sensitive to the idiosyncrasies of their rich Chinese clients willingly change unacceptable numbers assigned to them.

The telephone companies of Hong Kong are equally obliging. In Malaysia, Telekoms Malaysia is less tolerant of what they regard as superstitious beliefs.

15 BUSINESS INTERIORS

Today, the belief that good Feng Shui gives one's business enterprise a much needed competitive edge is nowhere more evident than in the design of office interiors, particularly in Hong Kong. Here Interior Design consultants are fully aware of the basics, and are also quite used to having their designs vetted by a Feng Shui man, like the local offices of international/foreign conglomerates and banks. Corporations like Rothschilds, Citibank, Chase, and even, the Wall Street Journal, all of whose expatriate Asian regional heads, I hear, consult the Feng Shui man whenever there are any reorganisations or relocation of staff, because this usually means a redesign of offices.

 LAYOUT OF OFFICES

Feng Shui for the interiors starts with the office layout and particularly the location and orientation of the office of the Taipan or big boss. He can be the President, the Managing Director, the Chief Executive Officer or hold any other title. if he is the boss, then the Feng Shui of his/her office has great influence on the fortunes of the business or company he manages.

The boss must sit in the most favourable, most commanding location in the office. Authority and power are the names of the game and according to Feng Shui this is usually that corner which is furthest away from the entrance to the office. By siting his/her office in the corner that is diagonally opposite the entrance, the boss will enjoy maximum control, concentration and good fortune.

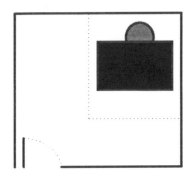

His authority within the company will not be questioned and his decisions will be well considered and augur well for the company's fortunes.

The *opposite corner* location is also the area where the source of maximum growth potential resides. It is also the place where *chi* is nicely balanced.

Boss should sit in the corner office

In offices where this location is not occupied by the *chief* executive then the person who does occupy it will enjoy good fortune, although this need not necessarily be good for the company's prosperity.

Access to the corner office should not be difficult. Outside desks occupied by secretaries and junior staff should be placed in a way which does not obstruct the flow of *chi*. This generally means that no one's desk should be blocking the route that leads to the entrance of the boss's room.

ALWAYS SIT FACING THE DOOR.

A very capable lady I know was experiencing endless problems in her small consultancy business. She had several things *wrong* with the Feng Shui of her office, but one of the most prominent was that she sat with her back to the door in her office. For the last two years she has continued to have problems with dishonest staff who constantly worked behind her back, stealing her ideas, her clients and recently even her money. Many things happen behind one's back and the symbolism attached to sitting with one's back to the door strongly suggest the occurrence of fraud and dishonesty.

For the manager who has his own private office therefore make sure your desk is placed in the corner diagonally opposite to the door, from where you have a commanding view of the entrance. Place your desk in such a way that it does not touch any of the walls so that *chi* flows around you while you work.

Desk positions should also be wary of having a glass window behind the occupant. To sit this way suggests a lack of support, a lack of protection for your back.

Offices with views are highly desired by most corporate managers. However views can be the source of malignant influences. It is thus advisable to examine the buildings, structures and landscapes that one sees from the office carefully. Views can also bring the glare of the afternoon sun and this is not good Feng Shui.

If there are sharp corners pointed at one's office, it is advisable to shut out the view with curtains. Likewise if there is glare although a wonderful alternative to this is the hanging of cut crystal balls which break the glare into rainbow colours thus generating good *chi* for the office.

If the views are of distant hills and pleasant landscapes it is good for the office. If there are waterways and lush vegetation outside the installing of mirrors to reflect in these auspicious symbols will do wonders for the Feng Shui of the office.

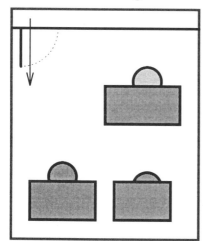

General office layout should also abide by the rules of Feng Shui. Thus desks should never be placed such that the occupants have their back to the entrance door. Indeed if possible everyone should have a good view of the entrance door. In fact one's back should never face a door, even if its the fire escape door. This is the surest way of attracting disharmony, dishonesty and bad tempers into the office leading to backbiting and a great deal of unproductive bickering.

This office layout is awful ! The staff sit with their backs to the entrance door; the desks are placed too close to the door, and the office itself is too small !

Desks should not be placed too near to doors either since this encourages absenteeism and clockwatching. Classroom style arrangements where a supervisor sits in confrontational mode facing the rest of the staff is also not recommended since this generates bad vibes. Where problems of excessive disharmony occur, Feng Shui recommends the presence of flowers, plants and even crystal (paperweights, vases etc.) which generally *soften* the atmosphere with *Yin* influence.

The most highly recommended desk arrangement for the general staff is the Pa Kua type arrangement, especially in small offices. This is where desks are placed at the diagonal, thereby simulating the sides of a Pa Kua. Such an arrangement makes for harmonious interaction between staff. It also brings good luck to the company and its business.

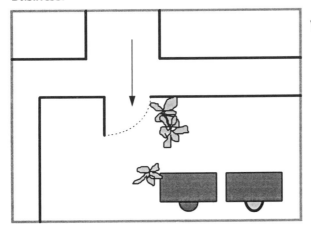

Where desks are in the line of attack from straight corridors or other malign influences like jutting corners or overhanging beams or facing a toilet door, the use of fresh plants works wonders in dissipating the bad *chi*.

Plants shield off bad chi coming from the corridor into the office

Crystals and windchimes are also effective cures, as are bowls of fresh flowers and even a goldfish bowl with live goldfish.

LAYOUT OF SHOPS & RESTAURANTS

For the layout of shops and restaurants, the most important objectives of good Feng Shui are the successful attraction of customers and the merry ringing of the cash register suggesting good business. Thus for these customer oriented businesses, the first priority is that the interior design must be welcoming.

Display arrangements should be done such that sales persons attending to customers face the door. Products must also be displayed in an inviting fashion in full view of customers.

Retail outlets should also be well lighted to attract a good flow of *chi* into the shop. The liberal use of mirrors is also recommended as this symbolises a *doubling* of facilities and products thereby suggesting abundance, space and prosperity. In many retail businesses these days, proprietors have found that the installing of fish tanks and small fountains to be good for business.

Restaurant owners, particularly like having fish tanks where expensive carp and other *delicacies* are kept live. These serve two purposes, one for Feng Shui as it is auspicious to have water, and the other reason is to demonstrate the freshness of the restaurant's sea food.

Modern Chinese restaurants are no longer as fond of reds and gold in their decor. And many of them have even done away with the coiling dragon which used to be such a popular feature of the older restaurants. Instead there is now the use of soft muted colour schemes, square as well as round tables˙ and a less crowded arrangement of tables to improve the flow of *chi* within the restaurant.

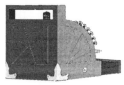

THE CASH REGISTER

This is the most important piece of furniture for any retail shop or restaurant. Its placement can lead to extreme good fortune or create disaster, and as such its placement must be done with the utmost care. This is because the cash register is the where all the money flowing into the business resides. The more auspicious its location the more *money* it will attract!

❋ Firstly the cashier must be positioned to have a good view of the entrance door. Needless to say his/her back must not be to the door. However the cash register should not be directly facing the front door but rather should be at an angle to the front door.

❋ Secondly, the cashier and the cash register must <u>not</u> be directly beneath an exposed beam since this creates problems and headaches.

❋ Thirdly there must not be sharp edges or corners aimed directly at the cash register. This generates bad luck and instability in the taking.

The cash register's good effects on the business can be enhanced in several ways, and many business people freely use the following Feng Shui suggestions which seem to have worked extremely well for many businesses.

<u>INSTALL A MIRROR</u>: Firstly it is very auspicious to install a mirror next to, or behind the cash register. This mirror has the effect not only of drawing in business but also symbolises the *doubling* of the cash register's daily intake.

<u>HANG A WINDCHIME</u>: Secondly, hanging a windchime above the cash register encourages *chi* to rise thereby bringing good business to the premises. if the windchime is made of hollow rods it is even better since this will generate healthy doses of favourable *chi*.

<u>USE A CRYSTAL VASE</u> Thirdly placing a crystal vase tied with a red ribbon next to the cash register also symbolises a smooth flow of business, fostering goodwill from satisfied customers which will make sure they return.

<u>HANG BAMBOO FLUTES</u> Fourthly some experts also advocate hanging a bamboo flute tied with a red ribbon above the cash register since this acts like a conduit for good *chi* flow upwards, thus increasing the patronage of customers. The flutes must face upwards, otherwise *chi* flows downwards making the business falter.

OVERALL CONSIDERATIONS

In addition to the specific guidelines offered by Feng Shui for orientation of locations, buildings, work areas, and furniture, it is equally important to ensure that the general feeling of the premises must be conducive to the creation, flow and movement of good *chi*.

This generally means that premises must be clean, have a balance of yin yang harmony and be properly lighted.

✳ Dark poorly lighted areas or corners cause *chi* to stagnate and grow tired, which will bring misfortune to the business. Good visibility and even non glare lighting within the work area are important aspects of Feng Shui which must be attended to.

✳ Damp areas give rise to rot thereby creating malignant *chi*. This causes problems and crisis to occur with frequent regularity.

✳ Areas hit by the glare of the afternoon sun cause damaging *chi* to accumulate bringing unpleasantness and bad luck. If there is excessive glare, the management should install cures such as anti glare glass, curtains or the hanging of crystals by the window.

✳ Lifeless offices and business premises lead to stagnation. An office which is too quiet and cold suggest bad vibes. Introduce some life with music, computers, typewriters clicking or live fish swimming in a fish tank. An office or shop which is too quiet encourages *chi* to stagnate which is bad for business.

✳ Ventilation of the premises must be efficient and at least some fresh air will do a world of good to the creation of *chi*. Premises that drip with dampness because of airconditioners continuously recycling stale air is bad for business.

* Valuable aspects of any firm's business (it could be the safe containing a stockbrokers scripts, a goldsmiths prize pieces, a bank's strong room, or a corporation's key manager or boss) should always get the good *chi* areas, i.e. those areas that are not too close to the front door.

* Plants introduced into an office, shop or business premise must be tended with care and should not be allowed to droop, die off or wilt. When this happens it suggests that *chi* has grown stale and lifeless. The same applies to the rearing of fish in the office. They must be healthy, and the water must be bubbling and clean. If fish begin to die off one by one, it is the surest sign that things are getting bad.

* Office premises must never be allowed to get smelly as the presence of foul smelling air creates bad vibes. Thus toilets should be located away from the general office such that odours from there do not enter the office. Unfinished food brought into the office should be carefully wrapped before being thrown away, and the office manager should institute an efficient garbage and waste disposal system.

* The traffic flow of the work area should be smooth and easy. Blockages arising from poor placement of desks or irresponsible dumping of boxes and papers is not conducive to the steady flow of *chi.* This leads to friction within the work area.

* Finally excessive noise in the business premise either because of blaring music or noise from the factory machines nearby or even worse, rowdiness of the staff create strong turbulence and is bad for Feng Shui. Such noise pollution often result in frayed tempers, low productivity and disharmony amongst the staff.

HOROSCOPE COMPATIBILITY
Since the smooth management of a business depends so much on its employees and staff, some practitioners suggest that to ensure compatibility and co-operation amongst staff, they organise their departments according to groupings of people with compatible horoscopes, thus strengthening team work within the company.

Suddenly the rain comes from the heavens,
The mountains bring water, the rivers and lakes fill up.
There will be a good harvest.

120

PART SIX

16 SOLVING FENG SHUI PROBLEMS

There are two ways of looking at Feng Shui.
One is the rational logical and sensible way which utilises the intellect so that as soon as Feng Shui problems are diagnosed, the thinking mind immediately offers a range of *"cures"* or solutions. For example if Feng Shui says we must guard against pointed objects aimed at our front doors then the thinking mind's solution is to try and block the view of such pointed objects !

Indeed, many of the suggestions offered by Masters of the art follow just such a logical approach, and thus appear sensible and obvious. It is common sense, many would say.

There is however, a second approach to Feng Shui and this often appears less rational, often even bordering more on mysticism than on rational thought. For example when there are problems at a business, the Feng Shui man could very well suggest changing the arrangement of the furniture, and Voila, all is well again ! The Feng Shui man brought in usually offers no explanation. In my long experience with Feng Shui experts, many are reticent when asked to give explanations for their recommendations, preferring instead to let you get the impression that he is mysteriously intuitive !

I of course much prefer the first approach. I believe and I know that Feng Shui is not difficult to understand or practice if we have access to the fundamental guidelines and concepts that make up the practice.. In short I prefer to use my own mind to think things through. I prefer to approach it as a science !

The sensible, logical approach to business problems and difficulties often call for an examination of the management, perhaps an analysis of the company's accounts, maybe the undertaking of an audit and so forth. It is the same with Feng Shui.

If we are convinced that many of our recurring problems are the result of malign forces created by bad Feng Shui, we can proceed to investigate how these malign forces came about ! And proceed from there to do something about it !

Hence a parade of dishonest employees, continuos bad luck, high turnover of staff and so forth can sometimes be traced to something being wrong with the Feng Shui of the office.

For those who DO believe in Feng Shui based on instincts alone, or are persuaded by its seemingly widespread and successful practice in places like Hong Kong and Singapore, and wish to make a study of the cures prescribed by Feng Shui, it is important to reiterate once again that Feng Shui has to do with *channelling, balancing and enhancing the flow of chi.*

This is the central concept of Feng Shui.

The philosophy behind the theory of *chi* flows, is that when one lives in harmonious balance with the environment, *chi* is enriched, enhanced and expanded. This in turn ameliorates the human *chi* flow within our bodies. The end result is vibrant good health, intense happiness and great good fortune and prosperity. In short everything proceeding smoothly and happily.

Obviously external environments for any one person are almost never perfect. Very few of us will be able to find the ideal site upon which to build the perfect house, in which everything within is perfectly aligned and perfectly oriented. Indeed if it were that easy all of us would be as rich as Croesus and as fulfilled as Buddha !!

To strive for as much harmony as possible however is another matter. It is possible to locate a fairly average location and build a fairly acceptable Feng Shui house, and where there are things that need to be adjusted, changed or altered, then Feng Shui *antidotes* can be brought into play.

I call them *antidotes* for in a sense this is what Feng Shui cures are all about, the antidotes that are used to counter specific Feng Shui problems. Often there are not one but several antidotes. One can correct bad alignments, poor shapes, wrong directions, stifling *chi* flows and all other ills, in several ways.

This chapter and the next summarises all the major antidotes used by Feng Shui men to correct Feng Shui problems. Once again to understand exactly how to use these antidotes effectively one needs to understand the central concepts of Feng Shui. Antidotes for Feng Shui can be categorised into three method groupings viz.:

THE CHANNELLING METHOD. This utilises the idea of pathways, conduits, and channels that allow *chi* to flow from the Earth or from the sky towards the site or house under consideration. This method utilises hollow poles, lights or pathways of any kind.

The idea is to tap into the Earth for *chi* to be brought to the surface, or to connect a place with good *chi* towards a place with no *chi*. The channelling method is the most useful method of correcting incomplete building shapes.

 THE BALANCING METHOD.

This is fundamental Feng Shui and involves bringing harmony to landscapes and surroundings. Thus houses that are irregularly shaped can achieve some harmony by the introduction of objects, like some architectural feature, some rocks or some trees. Balance suggests symmetry so that houses which are lacking in such symmetry will be made right with the introduction of features that balance the layout and the dimensions of the house.

 THE ENHANCING METHOD.

This involves adding specific *good chi* architectural features or other living commodity or object which can add to the Feng Shui of an area, by helping *chi* to circulate, or by dissolving *chi* that is too strong or even by creating *chi* in areas where it is absent.

Thus this method uses lights, fountains, fish tanks, windmills, bells, windchimes, mirrors and crystals ⁻ and a host of other things to *activate* the *chi* flows in specific corners and sectors of the home.

Usually this method is best used in conjubtion with knowledeg about other schools of Feng Shui thought. For instance if you analyse room layouts according to the Pa Kua method which categorises corners into different life situations you can use the enhancing methods to *activate* the relevant corners that will bring happiness into your life !

The enhancing method is thus especially suitable for the practice of Compass School Feng Shui. It is also a useful method for ensuring that there is element compatibility when objcets like windchimes and plants are used for the activation process.

Landscape Feng Shui on the other hand, basically utilises the first two methods. These methods are summarised in this chapter. Interior Feng Shui utilises the enhancing method and the antidotes for these are summarised in the following chapter.

17 CURES FOR EXTERIOR PROBLEMS

USE OF TREES AND PLANTS

Trees, plants and shrubs are perhaps the most commonly used and effective "solutions" to combat bad *chi* and by extension, bad Feng Shui. It is also often used to as a means of creating Yin/Yang balance because it is a living entity, thereby enhancing the Feng Shui of a site or location.

Trees are very effective in screening off poison arrows, especially those caused by straight, sharp or pointed roads, buildings or other objects. Trees are also excellent for blocking out highly undesirable or potentially offensive objects like boulders that are shaped like dangerous creatures and animals; cannons, flyovers that resemble a scythe or the sharp threatening corner of a big building, or even other trees which may be directly blocking one's front door and generating huge amounts of *sha chi*.

When arranged in a row to resemble hedges and "natural" separations trees can also serve a protective role to ward off bad and discordant chi caused by a multitude of bad Feng Shui situations.

In olden days, many villages in many parts of South Eastern China, bamboo groves were often planted at the rear of houses, and often, residents whose homes were built on completely flat level ground often planted trees as a substitute for the traditional protective hilly or mountain range.

Trees which are used as Feng Shui "Protection" should generally be allowed to grow naturally, without pruning or binding. They should be prolific growers, and preferably evergreen which represents abundance and prosperity. Vibrant green leaves are often excellent signs of good Feng Shui.

As a general rule of Feng Shui Trees planted near a building or home is always good Feng Shui, and especially so when they are planted at the back of a building. It is important to know however that they should not be planted too near the building itself. If the branches block out sunlight from entering the windows of a home or building, residents will suffer because the tree prevents *chi* from entering the home. There is another reason. Trees and plants are considered Yin and if Yin smothers out the Yang of sunlight there is no balance.

The rule to follow is to use your own judgement. When a tree looks good to you, feels right and appears beautiful, it is good. When it seems oppressive, threatening or completely cuts out the sun, it is better to have it cut down and to replant with new trees.

This often times happen in the Tropics where trees grow so rapidly, that it can happen that they become so big and thick, they end up *"smothering"* the home they were grown to protect.

Finally when Trees and plants show signs of rotting, or drying or appear to be dying, it is far better to have them chopped down and replanted. Rotting or decaying plants and trees generate malignant *chi* which does a great deal of harm to residents nearby.

* Trees as protection against harsh winds. When homes are built on hill tops, like this house here, trees can be planted where harsh winds blow, thereby affording protection to residents.

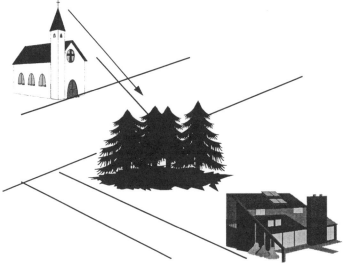

Trees block off effects of spire from across the road

* Trees as protection against excessive noise. Buildings that are located in the town centre and bordered on all sides by traffic and pollution can be protected by a row of trees which can *"shut"* out noise and pollution thereby benefiting residents.

* Trees as protection against pollution and foul smells. When the house is located next to a blocked up monsoon drain and there is a garbage pile near the back as well. Trees planted strategically protect residents against malignant *chi* caused by the foul smells.

* Trees as protection against nearby cemeteries. Homes or buildings which are located near cemeteries and graveyards can use trees to ward off the discordant influences.

* Trees as protection against straight "poison *chi* bearing" roads. In this example, shown below, the main door of the house can be repositioned to avoid the road pointed at the house but a hedge planted strategically gives further protection to residents.

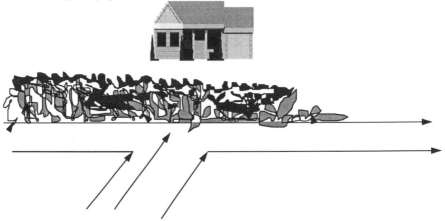

* Trees as protection against church crosses and steeples. Houses which face churches or temples can accumulate bad luck that come from funerals or memorial services held in such places. It is also believed that crosses create bad *chi* for those facing them. In this case (shown in previous page) therefore the trees planted in the compound of the house will protect residents.

* Trees as protection against knifelike road flyovers, which are fairly common in today's complex road systems. Tall trees with verdant foliage are especially suitable, and highly recommended for warding off all the inauspicious *chi* influence of traffic and noise.
Protection from a church spire

* Trees as protection against angled roof forms and lines. This is a common occurrence since most neighbouring buildings do have roof lines which can become inadvertently threatening. When this occurs, trees are an excellent solution.

* Trees as protection against telegraph poles, transmission towers, or any other object which may be pointed at one's main entrance. For example a tree can be planted to protect residents from a flagpole across the road.

* Trees can also be used to balance out homes and buildings which seem to be *"incomplete"* by having corners missing. Thus for example, an "L" shaped house (shown here) can be made *complete* with the tree planted in the missing corner This provides balance for the house shape ! Tree is planted here.

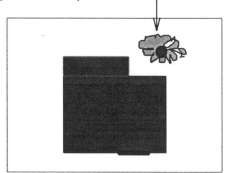
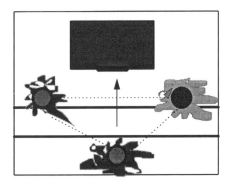

* Trees as protection against another large tree directly in front of the main door, which may be overwhelming the house with bad *chi*. In such a situation the most ideal solution, as shown here, is to plant two trees so that the three trees seem to form a sort of triangle pointing outwards. This dissipates all inauspicious *chi* sent towards the house by the offending tree.

USE OF WATER, WATERWAYS & PONDS

Water, in any form, almost always bring good Feng Shui. Water helps residents reach new levels of prosperity because water symbolises money. But water must be kept clean and fresh and flowing. Stagnating water, or water which is foul smelling is worse than having no water at all.

Thus if you had built a pool or a pond near your house and still suffer from a continuos stream of bad luck, check to see that the water is clean. In many homes swimming pools built in a flush of initial enthusiasm sometimes get neglected because of lack of use, or if the children have gone overseas to study. In such instances, either close up the pool completely or make sure it is kept sparkling clean and filtered.

The same advice applies for fishponds and little streams built with great enthusiasm when but which get dirty, muddy or murky through lack of care. Worse still if the water becomes dark and stagnant, it creates a great deal of bad luck and causes problems to the business and wealth of residents.

Water can also be used as a "*cure*" for homes and buildings which suffer from an excess of Yang objects. Thus, in cities and towns where heavy concrete and bricks dominate, a sparkling manmade waterfall, a pool, or a pretty fountain, especially if they are nicely landscaped with plants often bring good luck because they create good harmony thereby activating good luck *chi.*

It is necessary however to ensure that these "water" features are not too big or too close to the building since this then causes disharmony by having an *excess of Yin chi,* thereby dampening residents wealth and good luck. If this is your problem, it can be corrected in several novel ways.

If the water pool is too large, plant a tree on the other side of the pond thereby "extending the area of the house. ".

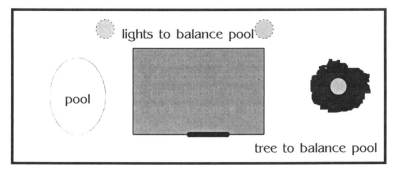

Pool too large for house is balanced by tree on the other side.
Lights at the back also balanace the pool being too near the house.

If the pool is too near the house, one thing to do is use an exaggerated curving pathway from the pool to the house to "*extend*" the distance, or easier still, install two spotlights at the two back corners of the house or building. In any case spotlights at the corners of the land on which homes and buildings are located is always good feng shui as it gives balance to the building.

* Fountains are excellent cures for buildings and homes in the city where there is too much Yang elements. When the fountain is surrounded with plants thereby good vibrant *chi* is generated for residents.

* Pools shaped in a way which allows the water to "wrap" around a house brings wonderful good luck, and is wonderful "cure" for those whose complaint is a lack of "money generating" *chi.*

USE OF LIGHTS

One of the most effective of Feng Shui cures that is recommended by Feng Shui experts is the use of lights. For external, environmental Feng Shui, lamps and spotlights, strategically sighted does wonders to elevate the luck of residents.

Installing lights at the corners of a land plot is one of the best ways of dealing with irregular shaped land, or irregular shaped buildings. Lights can also be installed to balance out "split" level houses.

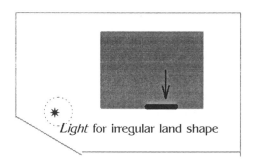

Light for irregular land shape

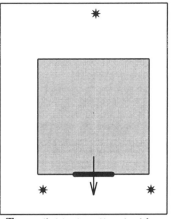

Three lights to attract chi

The use of lights work by "lifting" *chi* heavenwards, and encouraging it to rise. Thus to enhance the luck of a house, practitioners of Feng Shui often install two lights at the front, one on each corner, as well as a light at the back, often at the centre. By doing this, any miscalculation in the actual siting of the house itself is automatically corrected since the lights create balance for the residents.

Lights that are installed to enhance the Feng Shui of houses should shine at the roof tops.

* Lights provide balance for residents whose house is built either too near or too far from the entrance. In this example where the house is not sited in the "centre" of the land plot, the installation of lights soon corrects the situation.

* Lights can also be used to "balance" out land plots which are *incomplete* as is the case of say, L shaped land. In this case install a light at the corner facing the "missing" section.
The same method can also be used for an L shaped house. L shaped homes are generally not recommended. However for those already living in such houses, installing a lamp post at the *missing* corner does provide a good solution.

All other irregular shaped land plots can also be *corrected* by installing a lamp post behind the house.

* Lights can also be used to solve problems connected with narrow driveways. If the driveway leading to the house is too narrow, installing lamp posts along the driveway enhances the residents' good fortune. If the driveway is narrower in some parts install a lamp post at the narrow portion.

* Lights can also be used to *correct* a <u>wrongly sited pool</u>. Shown here is a pool, though in the auspicious kidney shape is sited wrongly vis a vis a the house. Such a configuration does not bring good luck, and indeed, wealth drains away. To correct the situation install tow spotlights at the two front corners of the house.

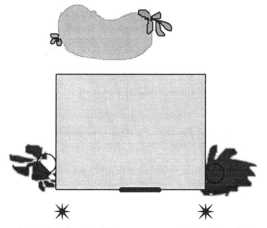

lights in front of house corrects badly sited pool

USE OF THE PA KUA MIRROR The eight sided Pa Kua mirror is one of the most powerful *"antidotes"* and protections for a household against malignant *chi* caused by external objects beyond one's control. It is also one of the most mysterious symbols used in the practice of Feng Shui.

The Pa Kua mirror can be easily obtained from Chinese temples or from shops which deal in paraphernalia related to the practice of Taoism or Buddhism. It is not however advisable to use the Pa Kua without consulting a priest or a monk at the temple as the Chinese believe that it must first be "blessed" by having certain mantras chanted on to it before it can be potent enough to ward off malignant influences. In Hong Kong the story of Bruce Lee's death revolves around the Pa Kua. It is said that Bruce Lee in calling himself the little dragon had angered the nine dragons of Kowloon. When told of this he arranged to install a Pa Kua onto a tree near his house for protection.

During a typhoon however, (no doubt caused by the dragons) this Pa Kua was blown away because it had not been previously "blessed". It therefore did not have the potency to stand up to the wrath of the dragons. Thus was Bruce Lee killed.

When I first arrived in Hong Kong, I lived in an apartment on the Peak which had a lovely view of the Harbour. In front of me however was the famous round building, the Hopewell Centre, which local residents told me caused bad Feng Shui for all those around it because it looked like a "joss stick". I was therefore told to install a Pa Kua mirror to ward off any bad chi emanating from it. I did this several times, but each time the Pa Kua kept falling off, a sign that it was not "potent" enough. Worse, I was constantly getting sick each time this happened.

Finally a local Feng Shui master arranged to install, not one but three fairly large Pa Kuas, hanging one from each of the three sets of windows facing the building. The Pa Kua had also been specially "blessed" at the famous Wong Thye Sin temple in Kowloon. Only then did the Pa Kuas stay up.

I do not therefore recommend the use of the Pa Kua mirror unless its installation in your house is done by a Feng Shui expert. It is recognised as a very potent antidote against "poison arrows" but its use can sometimes backfire, if not installed properly. This is because the Pa Kua, which derives its potency from the eight Trigrams drawn on it is believed to create certain vibrations which if not properly focused could do more harm than good.

CHANGING DOOR DIRECTIONS

One of the more drastic measures recommended to correct badly situated front doors and entrances is simply to change its direction. Sometimes this may be due to malign influences caused by any one of the "poison arrow" objects mentioned earlier. Sometimes it may be due to the fact that the direction of the front door has not been synchronised to match the auspicious direction of the head of the household. (✤ Refer to APPLIED FENG SHUI my second book on Compass Feng Shui)

If this is diagnosed as the cause of consistent ill luck, one way of combating it is to rebuild the front door such that it is oriented away from the direct path of poison arrows. Perhaps the most famous example of a change in door directions leading to outstanding good fortune is the story of the Hyatt Hotel in Scotts Road in Singapore. When the direction of all their entrances were changed, the Hyatt enjoyed a boost in its fortune which continues to today.

18. CURES FOR INTERIORS

With apartment and condominium living becoming more fashionable and common all over the world, Feng Shui attention is increasingly being focused on the interiors of homes. Room design, colour schemes, the use of *chi* enhancing objects have taken on new significance.

Interior Feng Shui has also become an important component of office design, furniture placements, and room layouts.

The many aspects of Feng Shui which need to be considered for room layouts, shapes and locations of important areas for the head of the household or the head of a business has been discussed in detail in previous chapters. Even if you are NOT the head of the house or of the organisation, the practice of what I term <u>defensive feng shui</u> can only benefit you.

These have generally assumed that the reader has full control over the Feng Shui of his/her home and office, although unfortunately this is not always the case. Oftentimes, one's room, home or office is assigned to us as a fait accompli. And sometimes one simply is not wealthy enough yet to afford the luxury of being fussy or choosy. Nevertheless, my advice is to do what you can, as best you can !

Accordingly we are addressing this kind of situation and focusing specifically on so called *"problem areas"* in Feng Shui. This chapter also suggests numerous ways of "enhancing" the *chi* around one's space, be it at home or at the office.

}Cures for interior Feng Shui generally dissolve bad *chi* and often enhance good luck by intensifying the flow of *chi* throughout the household.

There are fundamental panaceas to modify, mitigate, change or boost the *chi* around one's personal space.

Used with an adequate understanding of Feng Shui philosophy, these *"cures"* can resolve imbalances in one's home or office, and definitely expand the creation and movement of *chi* to one's advantage.

THE EIGHT REMEDIES

In my observation of Feng Shui practice over the years, I have identified Eight categories of Feng Shui remedies. These are:

* Bright, lighted things or things that reflect. Under this category are lights, mirrors, lead crystal objects, and crystal balls.

* Living things or simulations of living things. This category includes live plants, fresh flowers, aquarium or pond fish, small tortoises or artificial imitations of these things.

* Things that make pleasant sounds like windchimes which produce wonderful tinkling sounds each time there is a breeze, bells of all shapes and sizes, gongs and xylophones.

* Things that have a circular movement. This category includes pretty mobiles, windmills, revolving doors, miniature water fountains, as well as table and overhead fans.

* Heavy things that can simulate Yang objects like boulders, sculptures, stones and statues.

* Modern electrical products that can simulate activity and sound, like stereo music systems, radios, and television.

* Things that are long and hollow, like flutes, preferably made of bamboo, and modern wind chimes made of hollow pipes.

* Colours i.e. when used in harmony with the Chinese concept of the elements.

Each or any combination of the *"things"* listed above have unique characteristics which make them effective either in combating malign chi, or in creating good chi. Thus a revolving door or a windmill has the power to disperse the killing chi of a straight road or angled roof pointed at one's room or house. At the same time, the wonderful bamboo flute creates conduits for *chi* to flow smoothly past an oppressive overhanging beam thereby dispersing its stifling effects.

BRIGHT REFLECTIVE THINGS

Under this category are lights, mirrors, crystal objects, and crystal balls.

LIGHTS are lampshades, spotlights, crystal chandeliers or any other form of lighting. Use these objects to cheer up dark corners, stabilise rooms and create pleasing *"ambience"* within rooms. Lights are also useful for embellishing corners or areas of a room, apartment or office which correspond to the life situation that symbolises what you wish to enhance.

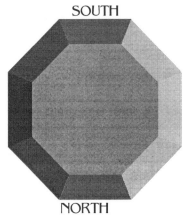

SOUTH

NORTH

Go back to the last section of Chapter Three where I have described the Eight Life situations of the Pa Kua. Superimpose these eight life situations onto a layout diagram of your home or office, and decide which of the corners you wish to intensify or activate. For ease of reference I have reproduced the Pa Kua with its Eight sectors in the diagram above. Their corresponding life situations are as follows:

SOUTH symbolises FAME, RECOGNITION, CELEBRITY STATUS
NORTH symbolises CAREER, WORK, PROMOTION POTENTIAL

WEST symbolises CHILDREN, DESCENDANTS, SONS.
EAST symbolises FAMILY RELATIONSHIPS

SOUTHEAST symbolises WEALTH, MONEY, PROSPERITY, PROFIT
SOUTHWEST symbolises MARRIAGE PROSPECTS & HAPPINESS

NORTHEAST symbolises EDUCATION, STUDIES & KNOWLEDGE
NORTHWEST symbolises MENTORS & HELPFUL PEOPLE

For example if you wish to stimulate your MARRIAGE corner, identify which corner of your home corresponds to the SOUTHWEST. This location in the home or apartment represents your marriage prospects, and can be activated, but first make certain that your toilet is not situated here, otherwise all your marriage hopes will be "flushed" away.

Toilets in the marriage or wealth corners could well flush away all the luck that the corner represents ! In ancient Chinese homes there are usually no toilets !

Instead, you should activate this area of your home with a beautiful bright crystal chandelier, making sure the chandelier is turned on nightly. If you cannot afford a chandelier, install a spotlight, or a bright beautiful lampshade. Or just place a natural crystal in that corner to symbolise the earth element. You can also hang marriage or love symbols in this corner. Paintings of lovebirds, or red threaded Chinese marriage knots or the double happiness symbol are also effective stimulants. Incidentally, good luck knots that are made of red thread are particularly effective for those wishing to add some zest to their dull social life !

You can do the same for any of the other corners of your home. Depending on what you want to enhance, just locate the situation you are most in need of luck for. Thus, using this method, you can actually enhance the Mentor corner, the Family corner, the Wealth corner, the Career corner, the Fame corner, the Children corner or the Knowledge corner.

These *"corners"* can be awakened and reinforced by many other Feng Shui *"amplifiers"* as well, and we will examine each in turn. Sometimes you can use more than one thing if you really wish for any particular corner to be activated badly enough. But the use of bright lights is one of the most potent methods. Personally, since I am very greedy for everything, I have systematically activated every corner of every room in my home !! Plus I try to use as few toilets as possible, and certainly the toilets of my home are NOT located in either the children or the wealth corners since these two aspects of my life are important to me.

MIRRORS are a remarkable *"cure all"* for a multitude of Feng Shui predicaments. Mirrors can deflect almost anything that causes problems for you, be it a threatening corner of a building, a straight road, or a garbage heap. Do this merely by installing a mirror and let it reflect the offending obstacle AWAY from your home. Better still if it is a Chinese type mirror enclosed within an eight sided Pa Kua.

Mirrors used can be any size if they are being utilised to undertake a protective function. Consequently even small mirrors can work some Feng Shui *magic.*

There are lots of other uses for mirrors inside the home or office. Generally the larger the mirror the better, and they should be in one large piece rather than be in the form of mirror tiles. In fact mirror tiles are very strongly discouraged as a design input This is because mirror tiles tend to distort reflections and this creates bad *chi.*

Mirrors should also be installed in a way which does not result in the cutting off of residents legs or heads. This symbolises an inauspicious effect on the health of residents, and is again, strongly discouraged. Thus the height of the residents must be taken into account when installing mirrors. Preferably mirrors should start from the floor upwards.

Wall to wall mirrors are encouraged by Feng Shui for certain important rooms like the dining rooms since this *"doubles"* up the family's food and by extension, its fortunes. Indeed you can extend this concept of *"doubling up"* into any area of your home. Do it with mirrors. You will notice that most restaurants and bars have full wall mirrors and this is to symbolise a doubling of customers !

Similarly a very popular practice is the installation of mirrors to reflect the business cash registers; in this case as a symbolic technique of doubling up the revenues of the business. Usually the cash register is located just inside the shop premises near the entrance. Install the mirror such that it reflects only the cash register but not the entrance door. This is a favourite method used by Chinese shopkeepers all over the world. The next time you enter a Chinese restaurant watch out for this feng shui feature !

Mirrors are also wonderful solutions to rooms which are irregular in shape, since placing a wall mirror on the *"offending"* wall gives it depth and creates the illusion of *"some more room"* beyond. Similarly, mirrors can expand a room that is too tight, broaden a corridor that is too narrow, and enlarge a lobby area that is too small. Mirrors on the ceilings of studies and offices are supposed to be good since it represents a *"reaching upwards".*

When there are <u>offending square shaped pillars</u> and <u>columns</u> in the home or place of business which sends out killing *chi* in four directions, wrapping these columns with mirrors dissipates all the deadly *chi* and turns a Feng Shui repugnant object into a pleasing one.

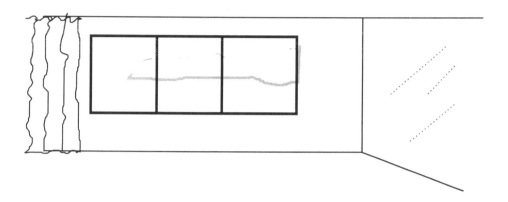

Floor to ceiling mirrors draw in water views into this room. Very auspicious. !

The most agreeable use of mirrors is that it can also be used to reflect into the home, any exterior view which represents good Feng Shui, like a view of water, a river, a stream, a pool, a fountain...or views of gently undulating hills that can correspond to the dragon. By reflecting beautiful landscapes the mirror symbolically draws in the good chi of the surrounding landscape.

CRYSTAL OBJECTS

The beauty and Feng Shui potency of man made crystal vases, paperweights, glasses and decorative objects make them extremely popular as gifts. Almost every room's Feng Shui can be enhanced with the presence of any kind of crystal object, and when combined with light, as in chandeliers they are particularly vigorous in creating good *chi* flow. Crystal vases containing fresh flowers are also purveyors of excellent healthy *chi*, and a crystal paperwieght placed on one's desk attracts good vibrations.

✳ It is worthwhile mentioning here that small faceted crystal balls similar to the type hung on chandeliers make wonderful Feng Shui magnifiers; especially when they are hung on windows which catch the sunlight.

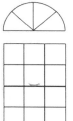
Hang faceted crystal objects near a window to catch the sunlight and create rainbows for home interiors. Very auspicious !

Faceted crystals break up the sun's rays into beautiful rainbow coloured lights, thereby converting strong *yang chi* from the sunlight into friendly luck bringing *chi,* and then disperse them throughout the *yin* room interior!

Hung on beams, such faceted crystals also encourage *chi* to rise, and hung on offending doorways (e.g. three doors in a row) they dissolve malignant *chi.*

In recent years, natural quartz crystals which have been cut into shapes of obelisks, pyramids, and six sided *"wands"* have also been used to enhance the Feng Shui of homes. These should be placed in the *earth* element corners of a home or room ie the southwest or northeast sectors !

Some practitioners also place these crystals on their family altars in the belief that these crystals have the power to enhance the blessings received from Buddha and Kuan Yin. Such ritualistic use of crystals however spring from spiritual rather than Feng Shui beliefs.

LIVING THINGS
Under this category are live plants, flowers and fish.

LIVE PLANTS always indicate good Feng Shui especially when they appear healthy, strong and verdant. Thus plants which thrive anywhere in your garden or inside the home or office are excellent indications of the presence of healthy *chi.* Because of this, it is imperative that if you see your plants suffering, rotting or drying off for whatever reason you must immediately do something i.e. to replace the plant(s) or to seek out the reasons and nurture the plant.

The presence of sickly looking leaves and rotting stems are the surest indications of bad *chi*. Dying plants or plants with leaves falling off are also symbolic of death, and thus are to be avoided.

For this reason imitation or fake trees, plants and even flowers are now extremely popular, especially the high quality imports made in the Philippines and Thailand where silk made leaves are carefully fixed on to natural barks and stems to simulate live plants. These imitation plants work just as well as the real thing and have the added advantage of not requiring excessive care and attention.

Plants are very dependable Feng Shui enhancers because they symbolise life and nature and growth. They possess the ability to conduct nourishing *chi* into homes and offices, and when placed at entrances encourage the inflow of prosperity bringing *chi*.

Plants are effective in correcting imbalances caused by protruding corners, free standing structural columns and sharp extended angles. Indeed they are excellent counter measures against any kind of sharp edges found around the home, edges that may be caused by protruding columns, corners, angles or pieces of furniture. The diagram here shows how the clever use of a plant hides a sharp corner while making the room more attractive.

In addition to plants, cheerful fresh flowers or their colourful man made substitutes are also effective in expanding the flow of robust *chi* within rooms. The international custom of sending flowers to cheer up sick friends is very good Feng Shui practice because flowers do attract a dose of healthy vigorous *chi*. Thus Feng Shui actively encourages the presence of brightly coloured, fresh looking flowers throughout the home and office.

Flowers are especially useful in activating the Family and Mentor corners of the Pa Kua life situation arrangements. Place a large flower arrangement in the corner of the room or house which corresponds to the Family corner if you wish to improve relationships within the family and to promote harmony in the household; or in the corner that represents Helpful People and Mentors if you wish to get the help and support of important and influential people.

FISH & TORTOISES

Like plants, these are symbolic of living things, and when kept healthy, alive and well in the home, they are regarded as being excellent feng shui stimulators. Miniature tortoises are especially popular in many Chinese homes as these creatures have a special place in Chinese symbolism. The tortoise symbolise long life and much good fortune.

What is significant is that fish and tortoises are creatures of water   that great symbol of wealth. We have discussed the magnificent Feng Shui properties of water (in all its forms and formations) and how vital it can be in enhancing the Feng Shui of the home or work place. If you have a pnd in your garden or an artificial one inside your home, do be encouraged to keep fish and tortoises in them. And if you wish you can also plant water lilies and lotuses (weather permitting). These too are auspicious symbols of happiness and good fortune.

Where it is not possible to have a view of water or the building of a pool in the garden, Feng Shui recommends the use of aquariums and fish bowls. In Hong Kong, the presence of live goldfish aquariums in homes and offices is almost a universal occurrence. Or if it is possible to do so, you can be really ambitious and look for the

ultimate feng shui fish, shown here ie the *arrowana* !
Fish symbolises many good things apart from wealth. They symbolise success at examinations and in careers.

A Chinese legend has it that the carp swims upriver, against the currents and upon reaching the *"Golden Gates"* it jumps over the gate and is transformed into the celestial dragon.

This symbolises the scholar passing the imperial exams and going on to a lifetime of wealth and success as an imperial official. The fish thus symbolises achievement, so that scenes and statues of fishermen catching fish are popular representations of attainment and victory. It is not difficult to find such representations in Chinese homes. Indeed Chinese New Year cards abound with *"fish"* and *"fishermen" symbolism.*

140

Keeping fish in an aquarium with its bubbling oxygenators stimulate the creation of *chi*. The fish swimming in the water also simulate life and activity, both of which are good indicators for business and commercial success.

In Hong Kong, Feng Shui men recommend the rearing of elaborate hybrids of goldfish. Specifically, one is told to keep eight gold or red coloured fish and one black one making a total of nine, the maximum number. The 8 gold fish symbolise growth, expansion and prosperity, while the single black fish symbolise protection.

> ....if you are intending to keep goldfish for Feng Shui reasons, the recommended number is nine, i.e. eight gold or red colored fish and one black one; this promotes good luck and gives protection at the same time...

The Chinese believe that when bad luck enters the home or office, the fish protects the residents by "absorbing" any adverse misfortunes. Thus, when the black fish dies, it is a sign that some accident or critical event has been avoided.

In Malaysia & Singapore the rearing of expensive Japanese carp, "koi" is a popular hobby, while many business tycoons go to great lengths to locate golden or red coloured "Arrowanas". These are the very graceful "dragon fish" which are also known as Feng Shui fish. They are mainly silver in colour and their natural habitat are the deep inland rivers of Pahang and parts of Indonesia.

The Arrowana is believed to change colour, into red or gold when tremendous wealth comes to its owner. This has resulted in ridiculous price tags being put on the Arrowana. Usually they are kept either singly or in groups of 5 or 9. I personally kept five Arrowanas which turned pink as they grew bigger and bigger in my indoor hall aquarium. When I left Hong Kong to return to Malaysia, I released them all into the Stanley Reservoir.

TORTOISES are also considered symbols of good luck. It is believed that the origins of the I Ching, together with its trigrams and hexagrams were first brought to the notice of the emperor Fu Hsi (the founder of the I Ching) on the back of the turtle. Tortoises are miniature turtles and they symbolise wisdom and stability. Keeping tortoises represent steady and stable growth, the enrichment of one's household. Aquariums, fish ponds and tortoise pools are best kept in the corner of the house or office that represents Wealth in the Pa Kua arrangement of life situations. When placed in this wealth corner, they enhance prosperity bringing *chi* and brings abundant money luck to residents.

THINGS THAT MAKE PLEASANT SOUNDS

This category includes windchimes, gongs and bells.

WINDCHIMES are amongst the most charming of popular Feng Shui objects. These come in a variety of designs and are made from metals, bamboo or wood. They are hung on doorways, along corridors and at entrances and give off a multitude of sounds each time the wind blows or when there is a breeze.

The most common are the inexpensive ones made of thin, light strips of gold coloured metal found in Chinese emporiums and temples.

These give off tinkling sounds as they dance gently in the breeze and are also the most effective, from a Feng Shui perspective. Hang them on offending overhead beams, or on doors to disperse malignant chi. Windchimes make good antidotes for such Feng Shui taboos as having three doors in a row, having doors of different sizes, having too many doors off a corridor.

More than being significant cures for problems, windchimes also enhance *chi* because the tinkling sounds symbolise the trapping of *chi* that is carried in the wind and allowing it to settle, thereby bringing good fortune to residents. Wind chimes made with copper or bamboo rods also symbolise rising *chi*. These hollow rods allow *chi* to be conducted smoothly upwards thereby heralding good fortune.

GONGS & BELLS symbolise the announcement of important events and happy occasions. Their presence in homes and offices are representations of the coming of good news.

In olden days, bells were hung on doorways and on top of lookout posts to alert residents whenever danger threatened. For this reason, they have also taken on meanings associated with *"warning"* and protection. Hanging a bell outside an entrance ensures that residents will always be forewarned before any crisis or disaster threatens thus allowing residents to be fore armed.

In modern Feng Shui, bells are not as frequently used as windchimes. Top business people sometimes place a symbolic gong in their dining rooms. In many of the homes of Hong Kong's wealthy tycoons for instance I have personally detected the presence of beautiful glass encased antique gongs.

These gongs, I was told symbolise the perpetuation of the family's wealth from one generation to the next and its presence in the dining room is supposed to symbolise the continuity of good hearty meals from generation to generation.

REVOLVING OBJECTS.

Under this category are windmills, revolving doors, fountains and fans. The revolving action symbolises the circulation of *chi* and these objects are particularly helpful in dispersing malignant *chi* which come from sharp angles and corners. In downtown Taipeh, in Taiwan you can observe many corporate buildings with large revolving doors. These, I was told not only attract good *chi* flows into the building but were also very effective in warding off and deflecting any bad *sha chi* which may inadvertently have been caused by sharp angled poison arrows from across the road caused by neighbouring buildings ! Revolving doors are very effective cures to counter any poison arrows that may be caused by long straight corridors or outside structures which threaten the entrance.

FANS are effective in preventing *chi* flows in the house from getting stagnant, particularly when there are corners which have been allowed to get damp or smelly from insufficient use.

FOUNTAINS almost always represent good Feng Shui and their widespread use in landscaping attracts good *chi* into buildings and for residents nearby. Inside homes and offices, the use of circular miniature fountains have been found to be particularly potent in creating prosperity and high business turnover for companies. Many investment banking firms from the UK and the US have installed these charming fountains within their office premises in Hong Kong and some have even extended the practice into the homes of their chief executives.

These fountains symbolise the *"circulation"* of water (money) thereby they are said to be especially good Feng Shui for banks and other financial institutions.

A few years ago, one of Hong Kong's most dynamic and successful investment banking partnerships was formed by four brilliant banking individuals and the giant Prudential company of the United States. Almost from day one the partnership has taken off. I had the good fortune of being their first successful *"deal"* and I remember observing the 12 inch circular fountain they installed in their entrance corridor. "Feng Shui", explained their managing partners ! Today the fountain is still there, while the firm itself has gone on to become one of the Colony's most successful investment bank and venture capital firm.

It is easy to install fountains within the home especially in the *wealth corner*. This is of course the Southe east corner of any house/apartment or room ! Go to one of the many landscape companies that have mushroomed in recent years, and custom made fountains can be easily designed to fit into the decor of your homes and offices.

HEAVY "YANG" OBJECTS

This category refers to statues, stones, boulders, and in fact anything which suggests strength and stability. Sometimes their presence in the home or office is necessary to balance a situation where there may be too much Yin influence. Indications of this are when things seem to be perpetually unstable and uncertain, or when residents cannot hold on to jobs or when one's employees keep leaving, or if there is constant bickering in the home between husband and wife caused by imagined or actual third parties.

In such cases, often the introduction of a statue or a sculpture can do wonders in curing the situation. Ask yourself whether the problem pertains to any of the life situations described in the Pa Kua arrangements, and then take action accordingly by putting a statue or a heavy object like a pedestal with a sculpture on top in the relevant corner e.g. if there are problems in the marriage caused by the husband or wife constantly having a roving eye, try doing this to the Marriage corner. Similarly, if the difficulty is one's career, placing something stable and solid in one's career corner will definitely help.

To those who *collect* those wonderfully beautiful statues of Buddha so popular amongst expatriates, some words or caution.
Firstly while it is excellent to have these Buddha statues in the home, they must always be properly placed in the home, i.e. they should be displayed in a way that residents do not *look down* at them. Elevate them if possible and if not possible, make them at least the same level as the residents in the house.

Secondly, be very sure of the background of *"antique"* Buddhas before displaying them in your homes. I prefer newly made statues. Because I can never know for sure the circumstances surrounding the journey of antiques from the temples of Burma, India and Thailand into one's home. And I prefer not to take the kind of risks associated with mysterious spiritual powers attached to things antique.

And finally, do remember that the Buddha is a Sacred Being to be treated with the utmost respect. One *"invites"* the Buddha into one's home. One does not *"collect"* or *"buy"* the Buddha.

MODERN ELECTRICAL GADGETS

Feng Shui experts move with the times and I have been told that modern inventions such as the Television, the Radio, and even the Computer can be excellent symbols for enhancing the Feng Shui of homes and offices.

These modern day contraptions simulate sound, life and colour and are thus excellent stimulants of the abundance giving and prosperity-enhancing *chi.*

Installed into proper corners according to the Pa Kua arrangement of the eight life situations, the Radio or TV can expand one's career opportunities, bring happiness and life into family relationships and marriage prospects, create golden occasions for generating wealth, expand the help from Mentors, bring success to one's Children and increase one's chances for Fame and recognition.

This, it is explained, occurs because these gadgets which use electricity tap into the vibrations of the Universe and are in tune with the energy swirls within the environment which create the flow of *chi.*

LONG HOLLOW OBJECTS

The most important object under this category are flutes or other things made of bamboo. For centuries the Chinese have played the flute which symbolises stability, peace and happiness.

When played, the Chinese believe the pure sounds of the flute lifts the spirits and morale of residents thereby bringing peace and confidence, safety and security.

Flutes made of bamboo are also believed to possess mysterious spiritual powers that enable it to enhance the *chi* of residents when hung in the correct way. This involves tying a red ribbon around two bamboo flutes and then hanging them at an angle facing each other, with the mouthpiece at the bottom, and simulating the top half of the Pa Kua. When hung this way on protruding beams they smother the oppressive effect of the beam, and when hung next to a cash register they enhance the income of the business. Bamboo flutes arranged this way are also believed to have the power to drive away burglars and attract amicable customers and friends.

COLOURS

The Feng Shui approach to the use of colours differs depending on who one talks to. For example the colour black is generally avoided because it is the opposite of light which is customarily considered the epitomy of good Feng Shui. Yet black also represents water which in turn, represents money. Thus black could be considered a good colour.

Again, white symbolises death to the Chinese, a colour of mourning. Yet white is also symbolic of light, which is good Feng Shui.

In researching for the definitive Feng Shui statement on colours I have discovered that the best approach is to go back to the basics of harmony, i.e. the harmony of Yin Yang balance; and also to apply the philosophy of the elements, the latter involving an investigation of one's element (i.e. depending on one's year of birth, whether one is wood, earth, fire, water, or metal) and then select the colour(s) which complement one's element.

> Thus black represents water, red is fire, green is wood, white is metal, and yellow is earth.

For general Feng Shui purpose it is safe to say that any colour which does not seem to be *"out of harmony"* is acceptable. And if you were born in a Wood element year, then black i.e. water is good for you. By all means then, use black as your dominant colour and you will surely prosper. In fact I know of a Wood element restaurateur who decorated his two upmarket Chinese restaurants in New York in combinations of black and who are still prospering.

146

On the other hand if you were born in a Fire element year then black (water) could literally be quite deadly for you. Avoid it. This is because water nourishes plants (Wood) but extinguishes Fire.

Generally, colours can play a definitive role in the manipulation of one's environment. In making choices, quite apart from the *"Elements Approach"* outlined above, it is also useful to understand some of the traditional connotations of colours.

Thus for instance, RED is the ultimate good luck Yang colour symbolising happiness, prosperity, fire and warmth. It is the colour that is principally used to attract good fortune during auspicious occasions. During the Lunar New Year red packets (called "ang pows" in Malaysia and "Lai See" in Hong Kong) are freely distributed to children and employees as symbols of goodwill and good wishes.

For marriages, the Chinese bride must dress in scarlet to attract favourable blessings from heaven; and the first month celebration of new born babies are celebrated with the distribution of red stained eggs. RED is therefore considered a `"safe"` colour to use for attracting good fortune, except when one's element clashes with FIRE which is symbolised by Red. For this reason WOOD element people should not have too much red around since Fire can destroy Wood.

Other *"lucky"* colours include golden yellow and green, the former because it represents the sun and the imperial families of China, thereby attracting brightness and high honours to the family; Green, because this represents Spring, new beginnings and periods of growth. Green is a Yin colour.

A word of warning about the use of colours for ceilings. Dark coloured ceilings are strongly discouraged especially if they seem to represent a "cloud" over the room. This often signals bad luck since rising *chi* becomes blocked and cannot circulate.

The flowers are moistened by morning dew,
The dry land is watered.
Everything is easily successful.

LILLIAN TOO

148

PART SEVEN

19. SYMBOLS & SIGNS OF GOOD FORTUNE

There is a great deal of vivid imagination and generations of superstition behind Chinese beliefs. This is especially pronounced in the wide spectrum of good luck symbols and prosperity emblems. Underlying these beliefs are ancient legends, village folklore, traditional practices, Taoism, Buddhism, Confucianism, and a vast history of recorded Chinese civilisation which spans at least 4500 years.

Symbolism in the Chinese sense pervades all areas of daily life. Every major life event, from the celebration of festivals to marriages, births, deaths, funerals... and permeating all aspects of the religious perspectives of their existence, symbolism is everywhere present.

Chinese symbolism could fill an entire encyclopaedia and it would still not be exhaustive. Within the framework of this book however, I have extracted some of the more popular "good fortune" symbols which have made their way into paintings, screens, sculptures, ceramics, robes, costumes and all kinds of decorative objects made from ivory, lacquerware, wood, jade and other materials, objects which can be, and are displayed in homes and work places in the belief that they hold the promise of attracting good fortune.

The practice of Feng Shui with its interpretation of landscapes, utilises symbolism in the interpretation of *"good"* or *"bad"* structural features. For households and work places, symbols of prosperity and good fortune similarly take on important perspectives, being excellent supplements to the practice of Feng Shui.

Hence most Chinese households believe they should have at least some of these symbols displayed in their homes. Good fortune in the Chinese sense, constitutes not just material prosperity in terms of wealth, but also encompass a good, long healthy life i.e. longevity; having lots of male offsprings to carry on the family name; power and authority; honour and fame in one's career and the smooth running of one's family and household.

There are a multitude of animals, flowers, fruits and plants within the Chinese pantheon which represent a variety of *"good fortune"* and displaying these symbols within the home or work place is believed to enhance the likelihood of such good fortune flowing to the residents.

In addition, the Chinese also worship a variety of Gods, assigning special powers to each of these Gods so that they may be protective or be the dispensers of wealth, health, heavenly blessings, longevity or courage, knowledge and so forth.

Included here therefore is a section on the pantheon of the more popular Chinese Gods, Bodhisatvas and Buddhas whose form and visage are displayed in Chinese households across Asia and in Chinese communities throughout the world as celestial and sacred symbols.

* THE FOUR CELESTIAL CREATURES:

The four celestial creatures are the DRAGON, the PHOENIX, the UNICORN, and the TORTOISE. These four creatures are regarded as possessing sacred and spiritual powers. They symbolise various aspects of good fortune. Their physical form, especially that of the Dragon is universally evident in many Chinese things.

Indeed, the Dragon is symbolic of the Chinese race itself and as we have seen, he also features strongly in Feng Shui symbolism. In fact Feng Shui is all about locating the Dragon and capturing the Dragon's cosmic breathe, the *chi.*

The DRAGON, or Lung, symbolises strength and goodness, courage and determination, bravery and endurance. He embodies the spirit of change, of revival. He brings the life giving rain thereby representing the productive forces of nature.

The Dragon is also the emblem of vigilance and security. Of all the creatures in Chinese mythology and beliefs the Dragon stands absolutely supreme as the most celestial of creatures, being the king of all the scaly animals of the Universe. He can live on sea or on land, and he can fly up to the heavens without wings. He can be as small as the silkworm, or as huge as the entire sky. But he is not a God, and whether or not he is a mythical animal or really does exist is not known.

But to the Chinese, the Dragon symbolises many aspects of good fortune so that restaurants and businesses use the Dragon as their symbol. His likeness is freely used in decorating their premises to attract good luck. For many succeeding centuries the Dragon has also been symbolic of imperial power so that the Emperors of China were likened to Dragons. Indeed in the great halls and palaces of the Forbidden City in Beijing thousands of coiling dragons decorate the walls, the ceilings, the doors and the thrones of the emperors.

It is understandable therefore that the Dragon is so popular today as a sure-fire symbol of good fortune. For those who want to know more about this creature, especially those born in the Year of the Dragon, I refer you to my book, "The Chinese Dragon", which I published in 1988.

In Malaysia, the Dragon symbol is also widely used. The Hong Leong Group for example uses the Dragon to represent the Group. Some of the more successful tycoons here also display the Dragon in their offices for good luck, like Tan Sri Vincent Tan, head of Berjaya Group. In Hong Kong, the well known Taipan, the late Sir Y.K. Pao used the Dragon to represent his new airlines, which at that time. was aptly named DragonAir.

The Dragon image is particularly suitable for those born in the year of the Rooster, the more successful of whom are believed to transform into the Phoenix, the natural *"mate"* of the Dragon. Indeed the dragon and the phoenix are depicted so prominently in Chinese literature and mythology that they take a premier place in the spectrum of Chinese symbolism.

The PHOENIX or Feng Huang, is the king of all feathered creatures, and is adorned with everything that is beautiful among the birds of the Universe. The Phoenix is believed to appear only in times of peace and prosperity. It symbolises the warmth of the sun, of summer and of fire. The Phoenix possesses the power to assist couples that are childless, and when its form is used together with that of the dragon to celebrate weddings, it signifies a union which leads to many healthy offsprings.

In Feng Shui, the Phoenix represents the South, and homes that are oriented to face the Phoenix are believed to enjoy good fortune for the South represents summer, warmth, life and harvest time.

The third celestial creature, the UNICORN or Chi Lin, is also a fabulous creature of good omen. It symbolises longevity, grandeur, joy, illustrious offsprings and wisdom. Sometimes referred to as the Dragon Horse, the Unicorn is said to possess qualities of gentleness, goodwill, and benevolence towards all living creatures. The Chinese believe that the Chi Lin ia always solitary and appears only when a particularly benevolent leader sits on the throne, or when a very wise sage is born.

The image of the Unicorn, either placed in paintings or sculpted as a decorative object, is believed to impart qualities of benevolence and wisdom. It also enhances the prospects of having filial and successful children.

The fourth celestial creature is the TORTOISE, which is universally regarded as a sacred animal. It is also an emblem of longevity, strength and endurance. The Tortoise symbolises the North in Feng Shui, and represents winter. It is believed to be immortal. Many myths and stories surround the Tortoise. For Feng Shui purposes, practitioners believe that keeping live tortoises serves a meritorious purpose, and because they are such excellent symbols of longevity, they are extremely popular with those who wish to live a long and healthy life.

ANIMALS THAT SYMBOLISE LONGEVITY

One of the most important aspects of good fortune to the Chinese is the ability to live a long and healthy life so that one is then able to reap the fruits of a lifetime of respectable living as an *honourable man* and more, one is then blessed with the extreme good fortune of watching one's offsprings bring distinction and esteem to the family name. Longevity is thus prominently regarded as being a vital ingredient of good fortune.

In addition to the Tortoise and the Unicorn, there are several other creatures which represent longevity. These are the BAT, the DEER, the HARE, the CICADA, and the CRANE.

BATS symbolises happiness and longevity. The origins of this belief lie principally in the Chinese word for Bat, i.e. "Fu" which also sounds like the word for "happiness". When used as an emblem of good fortune it is often painted red, the colour of joyousness. The Bat is strongly featured on Chinese robes worn by court officials, and is sometimes drawn so elaborately it often resembles the butterfly.

In ceramic ware and paintings the Bat is also often drawn in a group of five to depict the Five Blessings i.e. old age, wealth, health, virtue, and natural death. These five blessings make up the sum total of *happiness* in a Chinese sense.

The DEER is the only animal believed to have found the sacred fungus of immortality. It thus symbolises long life, and indeed the God of Longevity is always depicted with a deer.

Like the deer, the HARE is also regarded as a symbol of longevity, and when shown in red it is further regarded as a supernatural beast of auspicious omen.

The CICADA, an insect whose *"singing"* in the summer months is much admired by the Chinese, is regarded as an emblem of immortality and resurrection. In times past, a popular practice amongst wealthy Chinese was to have piece of jade carved in the shape of a Cicada and placed in the mouth of corpses before burial, thereby ensuring eternal life for the deceased. The Cicada is also a symbol of happiness and eternal youth, as it is said to be the only insect to live beyond seventeen years. Jade Cicadas are extremely popular with the Hong Kong Chinese since this tiny creature is also believed to inspire great ideas and represent vigour of thought.

Finally the beautiful CRANE, an extremely popular bird, widely depicted in paintings, screens and other forms of Chinese Art. The Crane is believed to be endowed with many mythical qualities and attributes, the chief one being its ability to live a long life. In fact the Crane is one of the most common and popular symbols of longevity. In paintings it is often drawn standing below the pine tree, another symbol of longevity.

The white Crane which also symbolises purity, is often featured on Coromandel Screens that are popularly used as room dividers by Chinese households.

ANIMALS THAT PROTECT

There are other animals which feature in the spectrum of important symbols and it is useful to understand their meanings in the context of Feng Shui. Some of these animals symbolise protection for the household, others are emblematic of endurance and courage.

Summarised in this section are the accepted *"meanings"* of the BEAR, the TIGER, the ELEPHANT, the HORSE, the LEOPARD, and the LION.

The BEAR is a symbol of bravery and strength, and the Chinese believe that hanging a painting of a Bear near the entrance of one's home is a potent charm against burglars

The TIGER symbolises military prowess, and is regarded as a figure of special terror to demons and cheeky spirits. Its form and image are generally used to scare off malignant wandering ghosts. The Tiger features prominently in Feng Shui, where it is depicted as the 500 year old White Tiger that copulates with the Green Dragon to produce massive amounts of cosmic *chi.*

Tiger symbols are often used with a great deal of care since this animal is extremely ferocious, being quite capable of "eating up" the residents.

Households which display Tiger paintings for protection purposes, must be careful to ensure that no members of the family are born in the years of animals which constitute *"food* to the Tiger, e.g. the small animals like the chicken, the rabbit, the pig and so forth. Indeed so strong is the belief in the ferocious nature of the Tiger, most mothers (of sons born in years that represent the small animals) strenuously object if they express the wish to marry girls born in "Tiger" years, believing the "wife" will surely cause the premature death of their sons.

Similarly most families actively discourage their married daughters born in *"small animal"* years from having a baby during the years of the Tiger, believing that the young infant, being a "Tiger" could very well swallow the mother in childbirth.

Having said that however, many Chinese strongly believe that the spirit of the Tiger is so strong he is one of the best symbols of protection against evil intentions from outsiders.

The ELEPHANT, though not widely seen in Chinese art, is nevertheless acknowledged as a symbol of strength, acumen, and wisdom. It is of course also one of the Seven Treasures of Buddhism, and indeed in countries like Thailand and India where Buddhism is highly popular, the Elephant is regarded as a sacred animal.

To the Chinese the elephant is also a creature of power and energy, and it is viewed as a an effective protector against deadly spirits. In the Ming Tombs just outside Beijing, huge stone elephants, shown in standing and kneeling positions protect the driveway to the Tombs, and one popular story has it that childless women often pray to these elephants for male offspring.

The HORSE is, like the elephant, also one of the Seven Treasures of Buddhism; it symbolises speed and perseverance, and Chinese households often compare clever children to young horses. The horse is not regarded as a celestial animal, but he is a popular symbol with the Chinese because of his noble qualities.

The LEOPARD represents bravery and martial ferocity, while the LION is an emblem of energy and valour.

Stone Lions are often placed at the entrance gates of temples and large family homes. They are perceived to be wonderful protectors of residences and public places, especially against demons and malignant spirits. In Buddhism the Lion is considered a saintly animal, and the Chinese often celebrate festive occasions with an elaborate Lion dance, complete with loud music. This is believed to "scare off" malignant spirits and bad luck, as well as to attract good fortune.

BIRDS that BRING JOY & HAPPINESS
In addition to the Phoenix and the Crane, other winged creatures also symbolise joy, beauty and happiness. Important amongst these are the PHEASANT, the PEACOCK, the COCKEREL and the DUCK.

The PHEASANT is commonly used as an emblem of beauty and fortune while the PEACOCK symbolises beauty and dignity. For centuries the brilliant hues of the Peacock's tail feathers have made them popular emblems of official rank especially, during the Ming Dynasty. Peacock feather fans are popular symbols which are often hung in Chinese homes.

MANDARIN DUCKS signify conjugal fidelity and happiness. These beautiful specimens of ducks are believed to be the most superior of their species, and are widely used by the Chinese to suggest romance and great happiness for young couples. Displayed in the home, they are believed to symbolise eternal happiness and bliss for newly married young couples.

The COCKEREL is regarded as a major symbol of the Yang element, and the Chinese believe that this domesticated bird has several virtues. The crown on his head symbolises his literary spirit; the spurs on his feet reflect his courage and bravery; the protective instinct he has for his hens suggest benevolence; and his reliable early morning calls symbolise his dependability.

The Chinese believe that a picture of a Red Cock in the home or work place is a protection against Fire, while a white one is an effective shield against the demons of the night.

TREES & FRUITS for LONGEVITY

There are four main emblems of longevity. These are the BAMBOO, the PINE, the PLUM and THE PEAR.

The BAMBOO plant is an all time favourite, and it is widely represented in art, poetry, and the literature of the race. The Bamboo is a symbol of longevity, durability and endurance. It is forever green and flourishes throughout the year. The Chinese also believe the bamboo possesses mysterious powers and that hanging it in homes wards off malign spirits. Bamboo, fashioned into windchimes and flutes is also considered to be purveyors of good chi and is thus widely recommended by Feng Shui experts.

The PINE is the most well known of all the symbols of longevity, mainly because it stays evergreen. The Pine is often planted with the CYPRESS tree, and because both these species do not wither, even in the harshest winters, together they symbolise eternal friendship which stays constant even in adversity. Pine Trees are extremely popular as subjects in landscape paintings and poetry about faithfulness and fidelity.

The PLUM, together with the Peony, the Lotus and the Chrysanthemum symbolise the four seasons of the year, with the plum signifying winter. Both the plum flower as well as its fruit are equally prized; the former is noted for its fragrance and purity, while the latter is so succulent, just watching it makes mouths water. The Plum is considered an important symbol of longevity because its flowers are observed to appear on apparently barren and lifeless branches, even when the tree has reached an advanced age. The Taoist Lao Tzu is reputed to have been born under a plum tree.

The long living PEAR tree is also one of the emblems of longevity.

FLOWERS that bring BLISSFUL JOY

There are five important flowers which have become firm favourites with the Chinese. These symbolise a variety of happy situations and good fortune, and are always displayed in homes during the festive season.

These flowers are the PEONY, the CHRYSANTHEMUM, the LOTUS, the MAGNOLIA, and the ORCHID.

The magnificent PEONY is highly prized by the Chinese as the King of Flowers. It is also known as the Flower of Riches and Honour.

Known as the *Mou Tan* which literally means *"male vermilion"*, the Peony is of the Yang element depicting Spring. It symbolises love and affection, and is the representation of feminine beauty. If the Peony tree bursts into full bloom, sending forth beautiful flowers and verdant green leaves, it is regarded as an omen of extreme good fortune. Thus Chinese households, especially when grandmother is still around, love displaying brilliant colourful paintings of the *Mou Tan* in full bloom. It is also a great favourite with aspiring artists.

Like the Peony, the CHRYSANTHEMUM is greatly esteemed by the Chinese for its variety and rich colouring. This flower is symbolic of autumn, but it also signifies joy and happiness, and is generally associated with a life of ease. The Chinese are especially fond of displaying rich yellow chrysanthemums during major festivals as the flowers are believed to create great happiness and joviality.

The sacred LOTUS has a very special place in the hearts of the Chinese especially practising Buddhists. There are wonderful connotations attached to this gorgeous flower which is often depicted, soaring exquisite and glorious from muddy murky waters, signifying its stunning purity in the midst of contaminated surroundings. The Lotus symbolises this purity, and also fruitfulness. It is the flower of summer, on which the Buddha sits and from which the beloved Lotus Buddha, Padmasambhava was born. The Lotus is displayed in households to symbolise peace and relaxation, as well as the escalation of spiritual consciousness.

Another beautiful flower, the white MAGNOLIA symbolises sweetness, while the exquisite ORCHID represents love and refinement. Both these

GOOD FORTUNE FRUITS

The PEACH, the ORANGE, the POMEGRANATE, the PERSIMMON, all have extremely good meanings. Each is exalted and loved for different reasons.

The PEACH is China's symbol of immortality, and the emblem of marriage. One of the legends of ancient China describe the Peach tree of the Gods that grew in the gardens of the Queen of the West, Hsi Wang Mu, and which bore the fruit of eternal life once every three thousand years. This was the fruit that gave immortality to the Eighteen Immortals, and the God of Immortality himself was believed to have emerged from the immortal Peach. Paintings which depict scenes from this tableau, or of the God of Immortality (Sau Seng K'ung) carrying a peach are popular gifts to the Family Patriarch as it symbolises the promise of eternal life.

The ORANGE signifies good fortune, abundant prosperity, happiness and wealth. It is widely eaten, given as gifts and displayed all over the home during the Lunar New Year, a time when the mandarin orange is viewed as "symbolic gold" by the Chinese not just because of its name, "kum" which sounds like gold, but also because of its rich golden exterior and the succulent flavour of the fruit.

And finally, the POMEGRANATE symbolises the promise of many offsprings all faithful and filial, and all achieving fame, honour and success; while the PERSIMMON, owing to its bright colour is a symbol of joy.

The Thirsty Dragon gets water;
Good Fortune has come.
Happiness reflects on his face.

160

PART EIGHT

20. PANTHEON OF CHINESE GODS

Chinese religious practice is a mixture of Buddhism, Taoism and superstition. The treatment of this subject within the parameters of this book do not pretend to be a theological study. Nor indeed is it meant to be very "*deep*" or very intense in the narration of the backgrounds of each and every Deity highlighted.

The pantheon of Chinese Gods is wide. Understanding them all involves an extended study. There are also "*overlaps*" of Chinese Gods with those worshipped elsewhere, by other cultures where different branches of Buddhism are practised. Hence many of the Gods, Buddhas and Boddhisattvas highlighted here may be represented in different forms by other cultures. Indeed the Bodhisattvas Kuan Yin, Pu Hsien and Wen Shu for instance, do indeed assume numerous forms, too many to mention. The Gods highlighted here are the more popular Dieties who are believed to bring good fortune, protection and prosperity to the home.

FU'K, LU'K, SAU.
They are everywhere, found in every Chinese household around the world, revered, worshipped and exalted. These are the three Star Gods; the most important, most popular Gods of the Chinese pantheon.

They are:
❀ the God of Happiness *(Fu'k)*, who stands a head taller than the other two Gods and who is always placed in the centre;

❀ the God of High Rank and Affluence *(Lu'k)* who holds a sceptre of power and authority; and

❀ the God of Longevity *(Sau)*, with his domed head, carrying a peach in one hand, and a walking stick in another, and accompanied by the deer.

Fu'k, Lu'k, Sau always stand together, and the three major aspects of good fortune which the presence of these Gods bring into a household also encompass wealth and successful male offsprings, prosperity and peace of mind, health and plenty to eat.

No right thinking Chinese home would do without these three Gods, which come in a variety of forms and sizes. Wealthy families often commission specially crafted giant size figurines of the *Fu'k Lu'k Sau* to display in special halls that have been designed to house them. Middle class families often display them as ceramic figures, beautifully painted in bright colours, and they are often placed on a high table either in the family room or in the Dining Room.

The Fuk Luk Sau

They are rarely worshipped at the altar with joss sticks or candles. It is enough that their forms are displayed in the home.

THE GODS OF WEALTH

There are several Gods of Wealth, but *Tsai Shen Yeh* is the most well known. His shrine is everywhere, and he is worshipped at temples. The God of Wealth is often depicted as two figurines i.e. one the Civil God of Wealth and the other the Military God of Wealth. The origins of this deity in fact go back to two mortals, *Chao Kung Ming* and *Pi Kan*.

Another variation of the God of Wealth is *"Wong Choy San"*. He is believed to be extremely generous to households which worship him. *Wong Choy San* is often depicted carrying a rat, with gold bars at his feet.

THE LAUGHING BUDDHA

This is the *Maitreya* Buddha, often referred to as the *"next Buddha"* or the *"Buddha to come"*. The *Maitreya* Buddha is extremely popular with the Chinese who believe that displaying his big tummy and laughing form is an excellent symbol of wealth and happiness. The *Maitreya* Buddha is often shown either standing with both his hands in the air or sitting in the Lotus position, surrounded by five children and laughing gleefully.

He is a picture of happiness and his big belly is supposed to contain much wealth. Stroking his belly at least once a day is supposed to bring good luck and seeing his countenance is supposed to make one happy. The Maitreya Buddha is carved onto ivory, bone, wood and jade. There are also moulded ceramics and lacquerware of this Buddha. It is believed that inviting him into one's home or work place creates good vibrations resulting in much happiness and wealth.

The Laughing Buddha

THE BUDDHA AMITABHA

This is the Buddha of Infinite Light, the Buddha who is associated with the Pure land or Western Paradise. The Buddha Amitabha brings a calm and peaceful life that is free of despair to all those who worship Him. According to the Chinese, the Buddha Amitabha preceded the Buddha *Sakyamuni*. His is the *"easy path"* to Enlightenment, and his two principal disciples are the Goddess *Kuan Yin* and the Goddess *Ta Shih Chi*. Households which display his form at the family altar are usually practitioners of Mahayana Buddhism.

THE BUDDHA SAKYAMUNI

This is Gautama Buddha whose teachings and disciplines include the Eightfold Path and the Diamond Sutras. The Buddha Sakyamuni is believed to have born in 560BC as a Prince in the Kingdom of Sakya, near Nepal. He left his family to follow a path of extreme asceticism, and one day, while sitting under the Bodhi Tree he achieved Enlightenment.

The Buddha Sakyamuni is widely worshipped by practising Buddhists in many countries, and his image is placed in a premier position in family altars to invoke his guidance and his blessings. Residents of homes where he has been *"invited"* in are believed to enjoy tranquil peaceful lives, with careers and business going smoothly.

THE MONKEY GOD

The Monkey God is acknowledged to be endowed with great craftiness and courage. Because of his inventiveness, he is worshipped as the God *"who can solve any problem and provide solutions to any difficulty"*.

The legend of the Monkey God is probably one of the most interesting and complex for not only did he at various times wage war against other Gods, he also accompanied the monk, Tripitaka in his famous journey in search of the Holy Scriptures.

The Monkey God is extremely popular with those who are engaged in businesses which involve speculation e.g. gambling, stockbroking and commodity trading, as he is reputed to give blessings related to solving tight situations.

THE BODHISATTVA MANJUSURI

Also known as the God *Wen Shu*, this deity is one of the Three Great Beings of the Buddhist pantheon. *Manjusuri* is the God of Wisdom and knowledge, symbolised by the sword he carries in his right hand, and the Book he carries in his left hand, even as he sits crosslegged in the Lotus position. Extremely popular in Nepal and Tibet, *Manjusuri* is believed to be the God who can purify minds and teach wisdom to the young child.In China *ManjuSuri* is often depicted, carrying the Book of Wisdom while riding the Green Lion.

THE GODDESS OF MERCY, KUAN YIN

Kuan Yin is the most universally loved and widely worshipped of all the Chinese deities. Her likeness, image and form are seen in almost all households, and there are altars dedicated to the compassionate Goddess of Mercy in very many Chinese homes. Shown here is one of popular representation of this much beloved Goddess.

Kuan Yin is the all Compassionate Goddess of Mercy. She is said to answer all prayers and to come to the assistance of those in need. Kuan Yin takes numerous Forms but to the Chinese she comes in the female form and is often depicted, standing or sitting, wearing a white robe and carrying a willow branch or a rosary or a small bottle of elixir.

Kuan Yin is also known as Avalokitesvara, (the male form) often seated with four hands, two hands in prayer, while two other hands carry the rosary and the lotus flower. This image of Kuan Yin is often invoked when help in the form of protection is required.

21. · THE GODS THAT PROTECT

Apart from praying for wealth, success and happiness, the Chinese also believe that all homes and work places should be *"protected"* from outside forces or malign influences. And the best form of protection is believe to be provided by their Gods, especially the God of War.

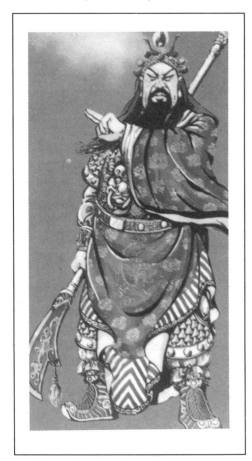

KUAN K'UNG

Probably the most famous and popular Deity for protection is the God, *Kuan K'ung* (also known as *Kuan Ti*, the red faced giant who is also the famous God of War. It is said that he is so fierce in his countenance that demons and evil spirits will not dare enter a house and into his presence if he is guarding the entrance. The story of *Kuan K'ung* has been well documented in the Romance of the Three Kingdoms. Today he is so popular that he is regarded as the patron, not only of the Military, but also of the Police, the Triads, the guilds and various other groupings of business people including restaurant and pawnshop owners, as well as antique dealers. Some Chinese also regard him as a God of wealth. *Kuan K'ung's* image is thus often displayed in the living rooms of Chinese homes, facing the front door so that all those who enter have first to pay their respects to him.

CHUNG KUEI

Often depicted in paintings with a barrel of wine, this Deity is regarded as a most effective exorcist. He loves to drink and more often than not he is drunk, but the Chinese regard him as an excellent protector against invasion by wandering spirits who bring bad luck to the home. Images of *Chung Kuei* are easy to obtain from Chinese Emporiums.

22. THE MEN OF WISDOM

FU HSI

Widely acknowledged as the inventor of the I Ching (or Book of Changes) *Fu Hsi* lived 4800 years ago and was the first of the Five Emperors of that legendary period. He taught his people to hunt, to fish, and to keep their flocks. He showed them how to build, to split wood, to weave and to play music. But he is remembered most for the I Ching, which has formed the backbone of Chinese thought throughout the centuries. Indeed the wise men who came later, particularly Confucius, made the study of the I Ching their life's work, believing the wisdom contained therein so profound that it prompted Confucius to remark that even if he lived his life all over again he would still not be able to fully comprehend the wisdom of the Canon of Changes. The image of *Fu Hsi* is rarely seen in Chinese households. However scholars hang paintings depicting him with the Eight Trigrams of the Pa Kua, to inspire them to greater wisdom.

CONFUCIUS, the SAGE.

Perhaps the most well known of the Philosophers of China, Confucius lived around 500 BC, and is remembered by Th. Chinese today as the author of the Analects and perhaps the greatest sage that ever lived. He taught that the nature of man was basically pure and noble at birth, but that it becomes corrupted by the impurity of his surroundings. Confucianism teaches that innate chivalry and lofty principles are the distinguishing characteristics of the highly moral person. Man must study the teachings of the Ancients and be well versed in moral social behaviour. Above all it is necessary to cultivate the Five Virtues i.e. benevolence, justice, propriety, wisdom and sincerity.

Confucius has an honoured place in Households which display his image as a mark of respect to his teachings. He is believed by the Taoists to be the "Honoured one of Heaven" who causes literature to flourish and the world to prosper.

Leaders of countries or large companies are believed to absorb in his wisdom by hanging a painting of Confucius in their study, or better still place worship him at the family Altar.

LAO TZU, the FOUNDER of TAO

The Founder of Taoism lived around 600 BC and got his name which means "old boy" because he was believed to have been born with a shock of white hair. Lao Tzu taught that inaction was better than action, that things would always work out without effort. "Let things take their natural course".

Taoism flourished because of the support of Emperor Shih Huang Ti who found the promise of immortality offered by Taoism to be irresistible.

Modern day practice of Taoism reflects many Buddhist rituals and ceremonies. Of interest is the Taoist view of Paradise, generally referred to as the *"Hills of Longevity"*, which are drawn as mountains, with lakes and streams, bridges and pavilions, pine and peach trees, and all the traditional representations of Feng Shui bliss.

Lao Tzu is not revered the way Confucius is. However Taoist stories about the Eight Immortals, the Elixir of Life, the Gods of Longevity and the Queen of Heaven provide interesting subjects for Screens, paintings and ceramics which are displayed in households as symbols of good fortune.

MENCIUS the PHILOSOPHER

One of the most important Chinese philosophers, Mencius lived around 372 BC. he was an ardent supporter of Confucius and he wrote one of the Four Books regarded as the Classics. Mencius was a Minister of State and reputed to possess a brilliant political mind.

CLOSING NOTES
. . . from the author

It's been three years since I began writing about feng shui. This was the introductory book I published to present this wonderful science to the world.

Feng Shui captivated me from the start In those early days, my perception was naively simplistic. It started out as a frivolous investigation into the promise of something magical. Just build your home according to feng shui, and , like waving an enchanted wand ... a lifetime of prosperity and happiness can be yours. With such promise, who could resist ?

From the beginning feng shui brought me amazing results. Soon after we married, my husband and I had lived in this rented house in Kenny Hills in the suburbs of Kuala Lumpur. We both wanted to start a family and looked forward to having a baby very much. Alas it was not to be. Despite countless visits to the doctor and faithfully and tediously charting my temperature each day ... it was to no avail. Finally we gave up trying and started breeding dogs instead !

It was around this time that we decided to build our own house.. By then I had become acquainted with feng shui, and it seemed sensible to consult my good friend who was an acknowledged feng shui Master. I told him that what we wanted more than anything was to have a baby ... I also found myself confiding about our abysmal failure to conceive. When he visited our Kenny Hills home, he immediately diagnosed the problem.

" *Hah* !" he told me triumphantly, " *it is this casuarina tree here that's causing you so much problem of course* ! " The tree, huge and massive and tall, was located directly in front of our main door, not ten yards away ! There was nothing we could do about the tree. We could not have it chopped down since the house did not belong to us.

But no more than four months after we moved into our new home, I discovered I was pregnant with Jennifer ! Since those days, several feng shui *si fu* have demonstrated to me again and again, the wonderful way luck can be improved with feng shui, not least helping me weather the bad times, and better yet, bringing glorious good fortune during my good years !

Deep investigation of this ancient practice has since revealed it to be a very complex wisdom. Far more profound than is at first evident. The study of feng shui takes one on a fascinating journey of discovery that blends several aspects of the Chinese cultural heritage. I observed that feng shui was actually an enticing composite of Chinese metaphysical beliefs and the Chinese astrological sciences, the juxtaposition of which presented immeasurable possibilities. I found myself swept into the realm of symbolism and superstition, philosophies and ancient wisdom. Thus did I enter into the world of *dragons* and *tigers*, positive and negative forces, yin and yang, energy flows, the cosmic *chi* and multiple interactions of the forces of Nature, constantly changing, constantly in a state of flux.

My preoccupation with feng shui had begun in the Seventies. I was learning kung fu from my friend and *si fu* Yap Cheng Hai at that time, and from him I had learnt all about the cosmic breath, and how I could actually activate my own body *chi* through meditation, postures and special movements, in order to gain internal strength.

In between these wonderful exercises, Master Yap told me fascinating stories about feng shui; its potent effect on families and households.

His stories were freely spiced with tales of prominent politicians and businessmen, those who had gained prominence and success, and how the good feng shui of their homes had enhanced their fortunes.

I became hooked on the subject. There were few publications on feng shui then. In researching the topic, I kept having to refer to books on related themes and it soon dawned on me that the whole spectrum of Chinese cultural practice (including feng shui) were inter related; that Chinese astrology, the I *Ching*, the cosmic breath, the elements, symbolism and so forth were all connected, and each had to be studied in some depth to fully understand the philosophy behind feng shui.

Thus began for me a passionate curiosity that has kept me captivated for the past eighteen years.

In the early Eighties I moved to Hong Kong. Plunged into this predominantly Chinese business metropolis, I soon discovered that everything Master Yap had told me about feng shui had been an understatement.

Feng Shui had an all pervasive influence over the people of Hong Kong and especially amongst the Colony's business community. Tycoon and taxi driver alike explained the booms and busts of the business world in terms of good and bad feng shui. Everyone, it seemed, including the *kweilo* expatriates consulted the feng shui man. Drawings of high rise buildings were carefully scrutinized by experts of the science before construction. Directions and orientations of offices and homes, as well as suitable dates for significant events were calculated by the *si fu's* who commanded fees by the square feet. Every now and again mistakes were made because of course, not everyone could afford the colony's best.

Even as scandals and financial collapses erupted around us in the terrible bust of 1983 following Maggie Thatcher's visit to Hong Kong, and the accompanying nervousness of the 1997 syndrome, (the crash of the high flying Carrian group plus spectacular collapses of several banks),

I heard countless stories of how the feng shui of personalities and corporations had somehow gone wrong. It was quite heady stuff !

I myself, from the vantage point as CEO of one of the larger local Chinese banks operating in that environment, was inundated with advice from my local staff to seek feng shui advice as a defensive measure against the difficulties of the banking environment of those days.

Because I am not one to tempt the fates, I took their advice and proceeded to look for good feng shui experts to consult.

The feng shui man whom I hired must have been good. Because my Bank went through that period of bank runs and economic downturn relatively unscathed. In the process I came to learn quite a bit about practical feng shui, especially since I accompanied the expert as he investigated every single one of my 23 branches, and got involved with understanding the reasons for all the problems diagnosed and the cures recommended.

I learnt about Pa Kuas (wooden ones and metal ones); about poison arrows; about mirrors and plants; windchimes; bamboo flutes; colors, placements of desks and furniture, goldfish bowls and water fountains and lots more !

In Hong Kong, I found it easy to find the books I needed; to talk to the right people and to personally investigate the gossip about feng shui narratives ... Hong Kong was a wonderful place to study other aspects of Chinese customs and beliefs, and I had the opportunity also, of visiting Taiwan and China several times in the course of my work, thus opening for me yet additional sources of information. On one of my visits to Beijing I went to see the Ming tombs, which it was explained to me had been built strictly according to feng shui. On another occasion I was shown how Canton had been constructed according, once again to feng shui precepts.

Sometime in the mid Eighties I decided to go into business for myself. I was most fortunate to find myself an exquisite apartment on the Peak, one facing the south (the more auspicious) side of the island. The views of the undulating landscapes were not just beautiful, they were also auspicious because they housed *dragons* and *tigers* !

Indeed I had found my *green dragon.*

Shortly after moving in, I succeeded in putting together a deal which enabled me to take control of the Dragon Seed department store group. The successful takeover of Dragon Seed was one of the most wonderful achievements of my life. I am convinced that in putting it together I had valuable support and help from my good feng shui !

Today I regard feng shui as an important supplementary management tool, something which everyone can and should learn.

No doubt my attitude has been colored by my exposure to the business people of Hong Kong who consider feng shui awareness as an integral factor of doing business. But also because feng shui has brought so much happiness and fulfillment into my own life. Not to mention all the help it gave me in during my corporate career days !

It is my hope that you, the reader will reap gains from your investment of time and effort in examining feng shui. Just a bit of advice. Feng Shui should not be regarded as a panacea for all your misfortunes.

Good feng shui can bring good fortune, even, incredible wealth ... it can vastly improve your life's circumstance. But it cannot completely change your fortune.

Life according to ancient Chinese wisdom is forever evolving, forever changing. We have our good times and our bad. Feng Shui cannot change your luck completely, but it can soothe you and take you through the bad times. And when you are living through your good years, correct feng shui will strongly magnify the good fortune coming your way.

As the I Ching says, *the Universe is constantly changing*. Man must live in conscious awareness of this changing nature of his environment. Only thus can he truly benefit from feng shui !

Lillian Too
Kuala Lumpur, January 1996.

THE FENG SHUI SERIES
by
LILLIAN TOO

The second book on Feng Shui.

Which reveals the secrets of the powerful
PA-KUA LO-SHU formula,
a potent branch of the Compass School.
The formula pinpoints each person's
four auspicious and
four inauspicious directions.

AND

explains how these can be
applied to one's homes and offices.

The highlight of this second book
is to share
a very powerful Compass School formula
that uses Compass directions

*to align individual chi flows
with that of one's surroundings*

*and in the process
tap into the luck of the Earth
and achieve abundant prosperity
and great wealth ...*

THE FENG SHUI SERIES
by
LILLIAN TOO

The third book on Feng Shui.

Puts the spotlight on
**PRACTICAL APPLICATIONS
OF FENG SHUI**

An easy to follow,
well illustrated manual
for those who wish to
seriously utilize Feng Shui
to enhance their luck
and their fortunes.

PRACTICAL APPLICATIONS OF FENG SHUI

**ADDRESSES COMMON PROBLEMS
FACED BY NOVICE PRACTITIONERS
AND PROVIDE ANSWERS
TO
A BROAD RANGE
OF INTERPRETATIVE QUESTIONS**

*a valuable easy reference manual
loaded with examples and illustrated
to answer your every question
on the practice of Feng Shui*

THE FENG SHUI SERIES
by
LILLIAN TOO

The fourth book on Feng Shui.

Introduces the
Time Dimension
to the Practice of Feng Shui

AND

explains the intangible forces
of the
Flying Star
School of Feng Shui

CHINESE NUMEROLOGY
IN
FENG SHUI

*explains the significance
of changing forces
during different time periods.
The formula highlights the influence of*
NUMBERS
*thereby adding vital nuances
to the practice of Feng Shui*

THE FENG SHUI SERIES
by
LILLIAN TOO

The fifth book on Feng Shui

An advanced manual on
WATER FENG SHUI
based on the Water Dragon Classic.
This book reveals the secrets
of the Classic and contains
the old formulas for determining
the correct flow of water.

When precisely oriented and built in accordance with
FENG SHUI calculations, the correct flow of water
brings great abundance of money and wealth luck.

WHAT OTHERS SAY .....

"... one could get hooked on Feng Shui after reading Too's books".
Book Review, New Straits Times

" LILLIAN'S BOOKS ON FENG SHUI
ARE CONVINCING,
THOROUGHLY RESEARCHED   HIGHLY READABLE
AND EXTREMELY COMPREHENSIVE ..."
YAB Datuk Seri Dr. Ling Liong Sik   **Dr. Tarcissus Chin**
Minister of Transport   **Chief Executive,**
Malaysian Institute of Management

"Lillian Too's remarkable books on Feng Shui reveal
extraordinary new insights ... and kept me utterly fascinated"
Atok Ilhan, Chief Executive
PHILLIPS GROUP MALAYSIA

"... the author's clearly written and
fascinating books ... are sure to make all who read them
look at feng shui with more seriousness and respect"
Karen Smith in B International, Hong Kong.

" ... NARRATIVE KEPT LIVELY   " THE PURSUIT OF
WITH INTERESTING ANECDOTES "   EXCELLENCE IS ONE
The STAR Newspaper   NEVER ENDING
STORY FOR LILLIAN TOO"
Success Magazine

".... outstanding and spellbinding "
DR Leong Yin Ching   " Lillian Too ... the woman with
the Midas touch.." Corporate World

*"... it is Lillian Too's considerable achievement to
have transposed the philosophy and practices of FENG SHUI
with such clarity, yet losing its essence"*
Book Review, New Straits Times

Lillian Too, a corporate high flyer until she called it quits five years ago, has
found a fulfilling career in writer. The author of eight bestsellers talks about her
passion for feng shui ... THE SUN MEGAZINE

Lillian Too believes in the harmony and balance of Feng Shui ...The lady is
something of a legend in Malaysian corporate circles ... Malaysian Business

Having gained esteem and experience in the corporate world quite inaccessible to
the ordinary person, she has now turned her hand to writing, and the art of feng
shui is right up her street ... *Corporate World.*

Everything around her ... is reflective of her warm, vibrant personality ... and though
she considers herself retired, to the readers of her best-selling books throughout
Malaysia, she's only just begun ... *Business Times*